KAL FLIGHT 007: THE HIDDEN STORY

by

Oliver Clubb

The Permanent Press, Sag Harbor, NY 11963

Library of Congress Number: 84-62522

International Standard Book Number: 0-932966-59-4

Manufactured in the United States of America

THE PERMANENT PRESS
RD2 Noyac Road
Sag Harbor, NY 11963

"What can we think of a regime that so broadly trumpets its visions of peace and global disarmament and yet so callously and quickly commits a terrorist act to sacrifice the lives of innocent human beings?

What can be said about Soviet credibility when they so flagrantly lie about such a heinous act? What can be said about the scope of legitimate discourse with a state whose values permit such atrocities? And what are we to make of a regime which establishes one set of standards for itself and another for the rest of mankind?"

President Ronald Reagan

"The enemy appears as the embodiment of all evil because all evil I feel in myself is projected on to him. Logically, after this has happened, I consider myself as the embodiment of all good since the evil has been transferred to the other side. The result is indignation and hatred against the enemy and uncritical, narcissistic self-glorification. This can create a mood of common mania and shared passion of hate. Nevertheless, it is pathological thinking, dangerous when it leads to war and deadly when war means destruction."

Erich Fromm

"And why beholdest thou the mote that is in thy brother's eye but considerest not the beam that is in thine own eye?"

The Gospel according to Matthew

For my parents, O. Edmund and Mariann Clubb

CONTENTS

ACKNOWLEDGEMENTS

I am grateful to the following people for the advice, assistance, constructive criticisms, or support they have given me: John Clarke Adams, Robert C. Aldridge, John Brule, O. Edmund and Mariann Clubb, Charlotte Cohen, Gloria Cox, Kenneth Dolbeare, Lesley Farlow, Paul Gordon, Richard Kram, Carl Marcy, Patricia Rector, Steven Soter, Edward P. Thompson, Kate Tomlinson, and Tobias Wolff. The support from some of those people has helped greatly to sustain my efforts and the advice has made this book better than it otherwise would have been. It should be emphasized that the conclusions reached in this book are my own and do not necessarily reflect the views of all those whose assistance has been acknowledged here.

I wish finally to thank Martin Shepard of *The Permanent Press* for his help in bringing the issues raised by the Korean airliner incident to public attention.

PART ONE: THE INCIDENT

1. THE MISSILE THAT HIT THE DOVES

There have been many times before our own when history, precariously balanced between peace and war, has been shoved by a seemingly fortuitous incident in the direction of war. We all remember such incidents: the sinking of the Maine, the assassination of Archduke Ferdinand of Austria, and the Gulf of Tonkin incident. In much the same way, the shooting down of Korean Air Lines Flight 007 over Soviet strategic territory in the Far East, during the early morning of September 1, 1983, came at a crucial moment in history—in our own times, a history in which the survival of the planet itself may be at stake.

Even before the KAL Boeing 747 was shot down, killing all 269 persons aboard, the trend had been exceedingly ominous. In August 1981, senior Reagan Administration officials had told the *New York Times* that it was the Administration's intention to acquire capabilities "to fight nuclear wars that range from a limited strike through a protracted conflict to an all-out exchange."[1] Then, the following spring, details of the Reagan Administration's "first complete defense guidance" leaked to the press—a long summary appearing in the *New York Times* on May 30. Tom Wicker aptly characterized the document, "intended to govern United States military policy for at least the next five years," as "a blueprint for turning uneasy Soviet-American relations into an unrelenting war to the death."[2] It was in such circumstances that powerful peace movements had developed in both the United States and Europe, offering a not unrealistic hope that the drift toward war between the superpowers— indeed, toward a nuclear holocaust—might be arrested. And it was in this context, just as the debates over the production of MX missiles and deployment of Pershing II and cruise missiles in Europe were reaching a crucial point, that the KAL airliner departed from its assigned course, overflew the Soviet territories of Kamchatka and southern Sakhalin, and was shot down.

In human terms, the downing of the airliner had been an awful tragedy. But politically, as CBS correspondent Bill Plante observed, the seemingly fortuitous incident had come to President Ronald Reagan as "a great political gift."[3] Indeed, it produced a dramatic political shift, both nationally and internationally, in support of the policies Reagan had been advocating. Speaking to the National Association of Evangelicals the previous March, the President had made clear what kind of consensus he was trying to achieve. He had deemed the Soviet Union the "focus of evil" in the world, denounced proposals for a bilateral nuclear weapons freeze, and called upon his listeners not to "remove yourself from the struggle between right and wrong, good and evil."[4]

But before the airliner incident such harsh rhetoric, and the Administration's calls for ever more armaments, had alarmed as many people as it had persuaded. "Until the KAL," a senior State Department official acknowledged, "Reagan was blamed for the bad relations."[5] Now, in the aftermath of the airliner incident, the President again took up the cudgels against the Soviets—in a political atmosphere which had been transformed. Addressing the nation on September 5, he charged the Soviets with a propensity for acting "against the moral precepts which guide human relations everywhere." And he called upon Congress and the American people to rally behind his efforts to build up America's military strength to combat what he called "the most massive military build-up [by the Soviets] the world has ever seen."[6]

This time the President found his audience far more receptive. ". . .after the KAL shoot-down," said the senior State Department official already quoted, "the President seemed to make sense to a lot of people."[7] So, too, a September 25 *New York Times* article by Steven Weisman was headlined, "Reagan Rides the Crest of an Anti-Soviet Wave." By Weisman's account, the President's advisers were confident that he had gained the upper hand over the Soviets "from what he repeatedly called 'the Korean airline massacre.'"

What the airliner incident did for the Soviets was the converse of what it did for President

Reagan: it gave them what a senior State Department official, recalling the event a year later, termed "a black eye of colossal proportions."[8] It "could hardly have come at a worse moment," observed the *New York Times*, "for Soviet efforts to generate support for the Western anti-nuclear movement and the campaign to halt American missile deployments in Western Europe this year."[9]

The incident also came as a rude blow to Western proponents of nuclear arms control. Murray Marder wrote in the *Washington Post* that, "The missile that struck the Korean jumbo jet scored a direct political hit on American 'doves'," providing "a classic example of how a single ill-conceived action by the USSR can rebound devastatingly on the American psyche and boomerang on the Kremlin itself." The incident had caused "instant, grievous damage to those committed to negotiations with the Soviet Union," observed Marder. "And the most intractable hardliners, who insist that the Soviets are beyond trusting, and are bound to violate every agreement with the United States, have received an injection of political adrenalin."[10] The immediate, practical results were much as *New York Times* columnist Anthony Lewis expected them to be—"to swing Congress behind even the most dubious arms measures: nerve gas, the MX, weapons in space. Resistance to the deployment of new nuclear missiles in Europe may weaken."[11]

It was not simply the immediate results which alarmed Western proponents of peace with the Soviet Union, but the ominous acceleration of a general trend in U.S.-Soviet relations. The sense of where things were headed was perhaps best captured by George F. Kennan, who wrote in the *New Yorker* of the "dreadful and dangerous condition" into which Soviet-American relations had fallen. Kennan noted the breakdown of civility between the two governments, the "antagonism, suspicion, and cynicism" permeating their reactions to each other, and the militarization of their relations "to a point where the casual reader or listener is compelled to conclude that some sort of military showdown is the only conceivable denouement of their various differences—the only one worth considering and discussing." And he asked, "Can anyone mistake, or doubt, the ominous meaning of such a state of affairs? The phenomena just described, occurring in the relations between two highly armed great powers, are the familiar characteristics, the unfailing characteristics, of a march toward war—that, and nothing else."[12]

Kennan also asked, "Is this state of affairs really necessary?" He affirmed, correctly I believe, that it is not. But if we are to arrest the drift toward war with the Soviet Union, we must clearly understand the processes by which we Americans, and the rest of the world, are being led in that direction. We cannot afford, at this critical moment in history, to keep plunging forward on a confrontationist course suddenly accelerated by patriotic outrage over the Korean airliner incident—without knowing all we can about an incident with so many unexplained elements. There may be a great deal more to this lamentable episode than the Reagan Administration has told us, and the whole truth could well cast the story in a very different light.

For this possibility there is a striking precedent—the Gulf of Tonkin incident of August 1964. Many readers will recall that incident vividly. The Johnson Administration, on August 5, announced to the nation that North Vietnamese torpedo boats had carried out "unprovoked attacks" against American destroyers cruising in international waters off the coast of North Vietnam. In the face of this "act of aggression," Congress hastily passed the "Gulf of Tonkin resolution" drafted by the Johnson Administration ostensibly in response to North Vietnam's "unprovoked attacks" on the American destroyers. And this gave President Lyndon Johnson a Congressional "blank check" to carry out an already planned air offensive against North Vietnam. The North Vietnamese of course denied Washington's version of the episode, but few Americans were inclined to believe the "Communist enemy" as against the story presented by our own President and his chief advisers. A handful of critics, most notably Senator Wayne Morse of Oregon and the journalist I. F. Stone, raised questions about the Administration's story, but they were paid little heed.

Only later, especially with publication of the *Pentagon Papers,* did it become clear that it was our own government which had lied to us. Only then did we learn that the Gulf of Tonkin incident had been deliberately engineered by the Johnson Administration itself as part of a

scenario aimed at creating a "nationally understood rationale" for its planned bombing offensive against North Vietnam. Only then did we
learn that the Gulf of Tonkin resolution had in
fact been drafted six weeks before the incident to
which it was the ostensible response. Meanwhile,
the American and Indochinese peoples had been
plunged into a greatly enlarged war which would
ultimately leave several million dead and
wounded.

What happened in August 1964 proves nothing, of course, about what happened to KAL
Flight 007 during the early morning of September 1, 1983. But why did this tragedy take place?
The only question to which we have a definite
answer thus far is, "Who shot the airliner down,
killing everyone on board?" But even here not
everything is clear. President Reagan, besides denouncing the Soviet Union for this "horrifying
act of violence," also asserted that Russia's behavior appeared "inexplicable to civilized people
everywhere."[13] On the surface, true enough. But
it is not only the Soviet Union's behavior which
seems "inexplicable." What caused KAL Flight
007's pilot to fly his Boeing 747 jetliner hundreds
of miles off course? How did he manage to evade
Soviet air defenses when his plane first penetrated Soviet strategic airspace over Kamchatka?
Why did he persist on this course, ignoring
Soviet jet fighters and despite the obvious dangers to his plane and its passengers? How could
the airliner's huge digression from its normal
flight path, overflying Soviet strategic territories,
not have been noticed by U.S. and Japanese

radar tracking facilities? Why were U.S. and Japanese authorities unable to warn the airliner—or why did they not choose to do so? These are among the important questions to which answers must be sought if we are to get to the bottom of the affair. Let us begin by considering the official explanations given for various aspects of the Korean airliner's ill-fated journey.

2. HOW COULD FLIGHT 007's NAVIGATION EQUIPMENT HAVE FAILED?

The region into which KAL Flight 007 "strayed," flying hundreds of miles off its normal course, is one in which there is a highly important complex of Soviet strategic bases. The original explanations given for this "accidental straying" were that perhaps KAL Flight 007's navigational equipment had failed and that KAL pilots have a propensity for "carelessness." But reporters immediately began asking questions about the navigational equipment carried by KAL's Boeing 747s. In New York, KAL's district sales manager told the *New York Times* that, "Since we skirt this area here very closely, the equipment we have on board is very important and very technical. It's a very difficult thing for that aircraft to stray." Ralph Strafaci, the KAL sales manager, said he could not elaborate.[14] But CBS Evening News, on September 2, and the *New York Times,* the following day, soon provided further details. On CBS, a pilot familiar with Boeing 747s said that such airplanes are equipped not only with the main navigational system but with entirely independent back-up systems which constantly cross-check the plane's course.

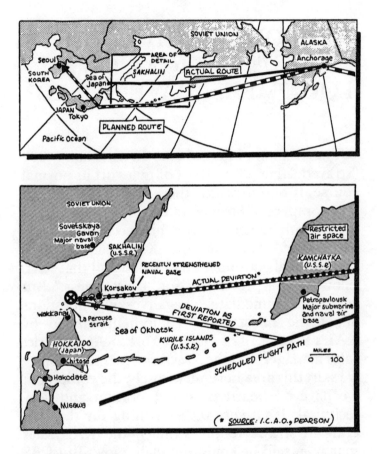

Maps: Paul Gordon
Sources: *New York Times;* ICAO; David Pearson, *The Nation*

The next day Richard Witkin gave a detailed description in the *New York Times* of how the navigational equipment on KAL Boeing 747s function as well as particulars about how airliners follow the route to which KAL Flight 007 had been assigned. Wrote Witkin: "The South Korean airliner that the United States says was shot down by a Soviet fighter was equipped not only with three computerized navigation systems but with radar that enables pilots to follow coastlines and other terrain features." Flight 007 had been assigned to route R20, "one of five routes established by international arrangements for crossing the North Pacific . . . Air traffic rules require that pilots report to traffic control centers when passing over six of the nine waypoints on airway R20." At Neeva, the third of the nine waypoints, the crew can check the plane's position simply by tuning in "the powerful Shemya radio station about 150 miles away. That will tell them the direction and distance of the plane from Shemya. And the crew can make sure there is agreement with the location given them by the self-contained on-board inertial navigation systems." Witkin's account made it clear that, given the nature of their navigational equipment and the several procedures available for maintaining KAL 747s on course, it was highly improbable that such planes could stray far off course through error or equipment failure.

When all this became evident, "U.S. intelligence sources" began putting forward a new explanation. As reported in the *New York Times* on September 4, these "intelligence sources" them-

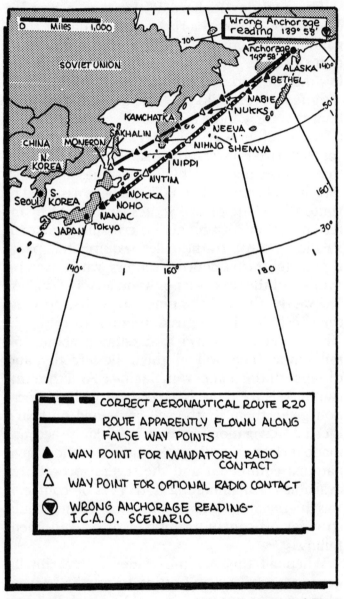

Map: Paul Gordon   Source: *New York Times*

selves now suggested that the possibility of malfunctioning navigational equipment was remote. A "senior intelligence official" observed that, "The plane did not veer off suddenly in some completely random direction. It was on the wrong path for several hours, never deviating from a line that would have taken it straight to Seoul."

This suggested, for the first time, that the airliner had not veered off its assigned course near the southern end of Kamchatka, as originally reported. But that was not all. The odds against Flight 007's pilot having done what the "senior intelligence official" said he had done without knowing where he was headed—straight for Seoul—are so astronomical that we can reject that possibility out of hand. Moreover, we can reasonably assume that the official in question wouldn't have made such a statement unless he had a factual basis for doing so; it clearly didn't serve the interest of a cover story. What this meant was that Flight 007's navigational equipment had been working properly and the pilot had known where he was headed. Quite evidently, he had intentionally adopted the new course he took across Soviet strategic territories.

Why had he done so? These same "intelligence sources" speculated that since this was the shortest, most direct route to Seoul, Flight 007 might have taken a "short cut" to save flying time. But KAL officials denied that possibility, stating that their pilots "were well aware of the danger of entering Soviet air space." Indeed, the U.S. Federal Aviation Administration supplies American airlines with a map warning in large letters printed over Sakhalin Island, where Flight 007 was shot down: "WARNING, Aircraft infringing upon Non-Free Flying Territory may be fired on without warning." KAL pilots are doubtless given much the same kind of warning. In the circumstances, the "intelligence sources" who put forward the "short cut" theory were obliged to admit that "they knew of no previous efforts by Korean pilots to shave flying time to Seoul by taking a more direct route" and that flying intentionally through Soviet airspace would be "unthinkable" to experienced pilots.

The pilot of Flight 007, Chun Byung In, had been a very experienced former South Korean Air Force pilot; according to KAL officials, he had logged 6,618 hours aboard 747 jet airliners. Colleagues said "he was completely familiar with Flight 7's North Pacific Route, having flown it from Anchorage for five years."[15]

It was against this background that President Reagan, in his September 5 address to the nation, felt compelled to give some explanation for Flight 007's strange behavior. Acknowledging that the 747 "is equipped with the most modern computerized navigation facilities," Mr. Reagan nonetheless affirmed that "a computer must respond to input by human hands. No one will ever know whether a mistake was made in giving the computer the course or whether there was a malfunction. Whichever, the 747 was flying a course further to the west than it was supposed to fly, a course which took it into Soviet airspace."

Thus, by President Reagan's accounting, there

either had to have been a computer malfunction or a mistake made in giving the computer the course. The two independently functioning back-up systems which constantly cross-check the main computer, designed to make a computer malfunction virtually impossible, had simply disappeared from the picture. So had the senior intelligence official's observation that Flight 007 had not gone off in some random direction but had flown undeviatingly "on a line that would have taken it straight to Seoul."

Subsequently, the International Civil Aviation Organization (ICAO), a United Nations affiliate, would undertake an investigation of the KAL airliner incident. At the end of 1983, it would issue its findings—again taking up the hypothesis that a mistake in programming Flight 007's computers was responsible for its flight into Soviet strategic airspace. We shall consider the ICAO report in due course. But meanwhile, the "navigational error" argument had already been seriously undermined, if not effectively destroyed, by the senior intelligence official's perhaps indiscreet observation. And that left the Reagan Administration without any very plausible explanation, to which it could publicly admit, for why KAL Flight 007 flew where it did.

We are also left with the fact that Flight 007's pilot did the "unthinkable." Given the obvious dangers to which he thereby exposed his plane and its passengers, we must presume that he had a motivation far more compelling than that of simply taking a short cut to Seoul. What could that motivation have been? The answer might

well be found in the fact that the line on which
Flight 007 flew for several hours without deviation not only would have taken the airliner
straight to Seoul; it also took the airliner right
over important Soviet military positions on Kamchatka and southern Sakhalin. If it was not an
accident that Flight 007 had gone off on a course
taking it directly toward Seoul, it is equally improbable that the pilot had, through sheer happenstance, gone off onto this direct line at precisely the point where it would also take the
airliner over these Soviet military positions. We
are justified in suspecting that this, too, had
probably been by intent.

Consider also the behavior of Flight 007's pilot
when the airliner crossed into Soviet airspace
over the Kamchatka Peninsula, at approximately
1 a.m. Thursday, Korean time. According to the
Soviets, when the airliner appeared over Kamchatka it was emitting "the short signals regularly
used for passing information on the radio-
waves." They attempted to contact the plane "at a
fixed international frequency, 121 megacycles,"
but the plane "did not respond to inquiries from
. . . Soviet control services." The Soviets there-
upon decided to force the plane to land at the
nearest airfield. "However, the intruder plane
was departing."[16] In the American account, the
Soviets scrambled several jet fighters to intercept
the airliner, "but a Soviet interceptor aircraft
never came closer than 20 miles to the Korean
Air Lines 747 as it flew over Kamchatka."[17] Thus,
the Russian interceptors never got close enough

to identify the intruding aircraft as a civilian airliner.

Nor did the plane identify itself when the Soviets attempted to contact it by radio. To be sure, it would be reported in the Western press, on the basis of information provided by Pentagon officials, that the radios on Soviet military aircraft are incapable of receiving or transmitting over the two international emergency frequencies—"to discourage defections."[18] But retired U.S. Air Force Chief of Intelligence Maj. General George J. Keegan, Jr. has upheld the Soviet contention that their interceptors are in fact equipped with radios capable of transmitting on such frequencies. Keegan, by David Pearson's account in *The Nation*, "said that he had personal knowledge that the SU-15 that shot down KAL 007 had [a] radio that was compatible with the 121.5 frequency."[19]

And Soviet air traffic controllers would certainly have been able to communicate on the international emergency frequencies. There is every reason to suppose that they would have attempted to contact the intruding aircraft on such a frequency, as they said they did, and that Flight 007 did not in fact respond. Moreover, the pilot of another KAL airliner, flying on the same route in the opposite direction, reported that he was unable to make routine radio contact with Flight 007—apparently because "it was having problems with its radio."[20]

But the airliner's radio was evidently working. Not only, according to the Soviets, was the plane

emitting short signals as it flew over Kamchatka.
The *Washington Post* reported that Flight 007
"made its five expected progress reports to Anchorage before switching its radio to controllers
in Tokyo . . . At 1:10 a.m. Wednesday (2:10
Thursday, Soviet time) Flight 007 called Tokyo's
Narita air traffic control center and reported,
'We passed safely south of Kamchatka.'"[21] That
last transmission would have been shortly after
the Soviets had tried, without success, to elicit a
response from the intruding airliner.

Why, then, did Flight 007's pilot respond to
neither the other KAL airliner nor Soviet ground
control? The most plausible answer is that he
considered selective radio silence necessary to
facilitate his flight over Kamchatka. More particularly, had he responded to Soviet ground control he obviously would have had to identify his
plane, and would have been ordered to turn
away or land.

There was further evidence that Flight 007's
pilot had not simply strayed unwittingly over
Kamchatka, but had overflown it intentionally—
taking pains to conceal his aircraft's identity. We
have this account from the *Miami Herald:*

> The pilot, Chun, appears to have turned off the
> signal device that would have identified him as an
> innocent airliner. It's called an IFF system, stand-
> ing for "Identification: Friend or Foe."
> The IFF is a transponder, requiring no action
> from the pilot, which automatically announces an
> aircraft's identity whenever queried by an auto-
> matic signal from air traffic controllers. The in-
> quiring signal incessantly asks, "Who are you?"
> and the aircraft transponder, whenever it receives

the controller's signal, answers with its tail numbers, airline name and flight number.

Pilots worldwide, civilian and military, American and Soviet alike, use the same IFF system and compatible equipment, according to several sources.[22]

By the *Miami Herald*'s account, Japanese military radars "reported a blip where Flight 007 turned out to be, but they did not report receiving an identifying IFF signal." Moreover, transcripts released by the Reagan Administration had the Soviet interceptor pilot saying, thirteen minutes before he shot the airliner down: "The target isn't responding to IFF." How can one explain the fact that Chun had not only failed to respond to Soviet radio inquiries as he flew over Kamchatka, but had also kept his IFF off until the very moment his aircraft was shot down? A veteran U.S. Air Force pilot told the *Miami Herald:* "Whenever you're off course and you don't want the FAA [Federal Aviation Administration] to know it, you turn off IFF."[23] Chun had quite evidently known what he was doing—and had been determined to continue on his errant course across both Kamchatka and Sakhalin.

President Reagan, referring to the Kamchatka phase of the airliner's off-course flight, would assert in his September 5 address that, "At one point the Korean pilot gave Japanese air control his position as east of Hokkaido, Japan, showing that he was unaware they were off course by as much as or more than a hundred miles." The evidence in fact suggests something quite differ-

ent—that Chun was quite conscious of what he
was doing, and falsely reported his position to
Japanese air traffic controllers.

Another question arises at this point. The
pilot, having overflown Kamchatka, had every
reason to assume that Soviet air defenses had
been alerted—even if he hadn't seen the interceptors sent up after his plane. Chun presumably
heard Soviet air controllers trying to communicate with him and knew, even while successfully
overflying Kamchatka, that his aircraft would be
tracked by Soviet radar as he flew across the Sea
of Okhotsk. He almost certainly had to know that
his plane would be in some danger if he again
crossed into Soviet strategic airspace. It would
have been a simple matter for him to veer slightly
to the south, over northern Hokkaido, instead of
flying over southern Sakhalin. Why didn't he do
so? We must begin to suspect that, dangerous
though it might have been, the pilot had a motive
for flying over southern Sakhalin.

In due course, we shall consider what that motive might have been. Meanwhile, what we have
done is to establish the extreme improbability of a
navigational failure of any sort. The pilot of
Flight 007 evidently knew what course he was on,
was determined to stay on that course, and apparently adopted various procedures aimed at
facilitating his flight.

For the KAL airliner to continue on that errant
flight, American and/or Japanese ground controllers also had to fail in their jobs—or acquiesce
in the airliner's flight. So let us now consider
what those ground controllers were, or were not,
doing.

3. WHY DID GROUND CONTROLLERS FAIL TO WARN THE AIRLINER?

What were the ground control stations which monitor civilian aircraft along the KAL airliner's assigned route doing during the more than two and a half hours when it was overflying the Sea of Okhotsk region? As we have already noted, pilots flying route R20 are required to report to traffic-control centers when passing over six of its nine control points—with control passing from American to Japanese control stations at a navigational fix southeast of the tip of Kamchatka.

At a dramatic Moscow press conference on September 9, the chief of the Soviet General Staff, Marshal Nikolai Ogarkov, asked some pointed questions about the inactivity of this control system during the KAL airliner's long off-course flight. Besides the obligation of pilots to report to ground control when passing the control points, said Ogarkov, "ground control centers have the obligation to consult precisely the flights . . . at those points." Why, asked Ogarkov, did the KAL airliner's passage through these points and then its absence from its regular flight path fail to "produce the alarm among the Japanese and American control services?" Why didn't the Japanese react "when the plane did not appear in their zone of responsibility on scheduled time?" Why did neither American nor Japanese authorities contact their Soviet counterparts "to prevent the tragedy?"[24]

The same issue was also raised in the West. As Graham Seal noted in a letter to the *Manchester Guardian Weekly,* the BBC program *Newsnight* showed that the aircraft "was being tracked in its flight by both Japanese and American radar scanners. Did they not tell the pilot he was on the wrong course? Why did two major powers using the most sophisticated tracking systems allow an aircraft to fly over such a sensitive area, especially when—again as shown on BBC—pilots are explicitly warned in charts of the area not to overfly it, or they risk being fired at without warning?"[25]

Assuming the BBC report to be accurate, it matters little whether the U.S. and Japanese radar scanners which tracked the KAL airliner's flight were civilian or military. The function of radar tracking, obviously, is to enable the tracking authorities to navigationally assist aircraft on their prescribed courses and to react to untoward events. The U.S. and Japanese radar alluded to by BBC did neither. Unless we are to assume incompetence, do we not have to assume that the authorities in question had unexplained reasons for not doing anything about the aircraft on their radar screens as it headed undeviatingly on its fatal course toward Russia's Sakhalin Island?

In the event, U.S. Government officials and Japanese sources in the United States told Richard Witkin of the *New York Times* that the

Japanese *civil* radar station closest to the area where Flight 007 was shot down is at Hakodate, at the southern end of Hokkaido; this radar station, they asserted, was too far away to have noted Flight 007's digression from its course and therefore could not have warned it.[26] This emphasis on the Hakodate radar station's inability to track aircraft beyond its range leads us away from the question of the air traffic control facilities responsible for monitoring the airliner's flight *had it stayed on course.* Flight 007 obviously didn't appear where it was supposed to be—indeed, it was long overdue. In these circumstances, as the *San Francisco Examiner and Chronicle* noted, "The pilot told Tokyo controllers he was 113 miles southeast of Japan's northernmost island of Hokkaido—if true, where his position would have been displayed on controllers' radar screens—when in fact he was hundreds of miles north of that position."[27] Thus, air traffic controllers at Tokyo's Narita airport and the radar operators at Hakodate could not have failed to discover that Flight 007 was not where it was supposed to be, and nowhere near where its pilot reported it to be. Yet, from what we have been told, they issued no warning to Flight 007's pilot. How can this be explained away? Can we not reasonably conclude that the airliner's errant flight was allowed to continue because it was off course by intent, and that Japanese air controllers had been induced to cooperate?

And why have the transcripts of radio conversations between Japanese air traffic controllers and Flight 007's pilot, which would have oc-

curred in accordance with normal flight procedures, not been released? The taped transcript of
one such conversation, just before Flight 007 was
shot down, was released by the Reagan Administration; and Jeane J. Kirkpatrick, chief U.S. dele-
gate to the United Nations, told reporters that
the full taped transcripts of conversations between the KAL crew and Japanese ground controllers would be made public, as Witkin reported on September 8, "this week." The U.S.
State Department then explained that the tapes
were controlled by the Japanese Ministry of
Transportation, which would make any decisions
about their release. As Witkin noted, the
transcripts of these conversations are a "vital
piece of the puzzle" which might "throw light on
when and why the plane veered off course."
They surely would have been quickly released
had they substantiated the official explanations
for the KAL airliner's errant flight. Yet the
transcripts were never released. One must
strongly suspect, therefore, that the tapes were
withheld because they contained material which
would have undermined those official explanations.

At bottom, the assertion that the KAL airliner's
deviant flight went undetected for two and a half
hours by U.S. and Japanese ground control authorities rests on the idea that the sophisticated
ground control system created to monitor flights
along this extremely sensitive route was incapable, though it employed the most sophisticated
equipment available, of doing what it was designed to do. That seems almost inconceivable on

the face on it. It is far more likely that ground controllers in fact noted that something was very much amiss and that Flight 007 was not rerouted away from its deviant course for reasons which could not be publicly given. The fact that the tapes of the radio conversations discussed above were not released lends further support to this conclusion.

4. WHAT DID U.S. INTELLIGENCE KNOW—AND DO?

We are not yet finished with the question of what was known on the Western side—especially by U.S. intelligence. On the morning of September 1, soon after Flight 007 was shot down, Secretary of State George P. Shultz and Assistant Secretary of State Richard Burt held a news conference at which they were able to give what the *New York Times* called "unusually detailed descriptions of the events of the last 24 hours." But Mr. Burt also contended that the United States did not have "real-time information" about the flight and that such information had to be retrieved and translated—with "intelligence experts" asserting that the Koreans and Japanese had "more concentrated intelligence efforts in regions abutting their territory than does the United States." Mr. Shultz, for his part, reported that Soviet radar had tracked Flight 007 "for some two and a half hours"—from the time it approached Kamchatka; but there was no acknowledgement that, as BBC reported, the flight had also been tracked by Japanese and American radar.[28] The effect of these explanations, of course, was to absolve the United States of responsibility for knowing anything about Flight 007's two and a half hour flight to disaster while it was going on and of doing something to get the airliner off its course.

But how was it that U.S. intelligence would not have tracked Flight 007 as soon as it strayed from its flight path into Soviet airspace, or tracked the Soviet jet fighters sent up to intercept it? In fact, the United States had constructed a global electronic intelligence network which, as the *New York Times* noted, included 4,120 National Security Agency (NSA) intercept stations scattered around the world as long as a quarter of a century ago. "Since then, with the development of surveillance satellites, the ability of military intelligence to track aircraft movements and intercept messages has increased many fold. For the past three decades, military intelligence officials routinely have followed the passive radar emissions of both military and commercial aircraft, even on the ground, from as far as 10,000 miles away." The *Times* also noted the strategic significance of the region into which Flight 007 strayed: "Sakhalin is a pivot of Soviet defenses in the Far East, which include the bases of the Soviet Pacific Fleet and a ring of combat air bases." Moreover, "United States surveillance of Soviet activities in the area rests on a communications Security Group based in northern Hokkaido"— directly across La Perouse Strait from Sakhalin. And finally, for more than thirty years, there has been an "aggressive American effort to develop technical intelligence penetration of the Sea of Okhotsk . . ."[29]

These operations have been described in considerable detail by James Bamford in his book about the National Security Agency (NSA), *The Puzzle Palace*. His account tells us much about the nature of this "aggressive" American intelligence effort, and about U.S. intelligence capabilities. Thus, wrote Bamford, the NSA has been "ferreting" the Soviet border for many years, with aircraft jam-packed "with the latest in electronic and communications gear." These aircraft, flying parallel to the Russian border, would pick up the emissions from air defense radar, ground communications and microwave signals for transmission to NSA for analysis. "But there was one major handicap: only that radar which is activated can be captured, and some of the most important radar [that associated with air defense systems] became activated only by a border penetration." Therefore, military aircraft on NSA missions sometimes "engaged in the dangerous game of 'fox and hounds'"—flying directly toward the Russian border to activate Soviet radar and pulling back at the last minute, or, on occasion, actually penetrating Soviet airspace.[30]

As a result of these activities, quite a few American aircraft were shot down—a Navy patrol bomber flying over the Baltic in 1950, another Navy bomber on a reconnaissance mission off Siberia the following year, and, that same year, an Air Force Superfortress on a reconnaissance flight which was shot down over the Sea of Japan. "One of the luckier missions," wrote Bamford, "took place on March 15, 1953, when a four-engine American reconnaissance plane flying twenty-five miles off the Soviet coast, a hundred miles northeast of the giant Soviet naval base of Petropavlovsk on the Kamchatka Peninsula, was set on by two MIGs." One of the two MIGs opened fire but the American "ferret" aircraft, returning fire, made it safely back to Elmendorf Air Force Base in Alaska.[31]

It is clear from Bamford's account that many of these operations were concentrated in the important strategic region into which KAL Flight 007 ostensibly "strayed" in September 1983, to be shot down by a Soviet jet fighter. On September 4, 1954, a Navy bomber on a reconnaissance flight from Atsugi, Japan, was shot down off the Siberian coast by Soviet interceptors, with one flier killed; and only two months later another reconnaissance aircraft was shot down not far from Hokkaido, also with one man killed. Precisely where such aircraft were when they were attacked is not easy to determine: whether they penetrated Soviet airspace or not, Washington would quite naturally claim that they had been flying over international waters on routine reconnaissance missions.

But on September 2, 1958, an American EC-130 was unable to make it back after crossing from Turkey into Soviet airspace. The aircraft was attacked by Russian jet fighters and crashed in the mountains of Soviet Armenia, killing six crew members. The mission had been monitored by a U.S. electronic intelligence listening post at Trabzon, Turkey; and from what they heard, U.S. officials concluded that the eleven other crew members had bailed out safely. The effort to get those crew members back tells us much about the thoroughness with which NSA listening stations were monitoring Soviet military communications as long as a quarter of a century ago.

President Dwight D. Eisenhower, by Bamford's account, "knew exactly what had happened and why; he had probably even read the intercepted conversations of the MIG attackers. But to reveal this knowledge would be to tell Russia and the world that American intelligence continuously eavesdrops on the Soviet Union." The Eisenhower Administration nonetheless decided, by way of trying to get the missing crewmen back, "to take an unprecedented and calculated risk: to reveal secretly to Soviet officials the intercepted conversations of their own MIG pilots." Meeting in his office with Soviet Ambassador Mikhail A. Menshikov and the Soviet air attache, Major General Mikhail N. Kostiouk, Under Secretary of State Robert Murphy offered to play for the Soviet officials "the actual tape of the intercepted conversations between the Soviet pilots who shot down the EC-130." The "startled" Menshikov refused to listen and Murphy's demands for information elicited only denials.

Then, on February 6, 1959, less than three months before Francis Gary Powers took off on his ill-fated U-2 flight over the Soviet Union, Secretary of State John Foster Dulles released to the press "a complete translation of the intercepted conversations between the MIG pilots just before, during, and immediately after the attack on the aircraft." Dulles did not reveal how the U.S. had obtained the recorded conversations; and the Soviets, publicly confronted with evidence that MIG fighters had shot down the "straying" American aircraft, denounced the translation as a "gross forgery." The U.S. Government was never able to discover what had happened to the eleven missing crewmen and in 1962 they were officially pronounced "presumed dead."[32]

Bamford's account tells us several things. To begin with, he provides us with a clear picture of the "secret and bloody war" which has been raging for decades in the highly sensitive Soviet strategic region into which KAL Flight 007 strayed—giving us a much better sense of the context in which that ostensibly accidental event took place. Secondly, his account of the EC-130's ill-fated flight makes it clear that, as early as 1958, American capabilities for monitoring Soviet air defense communications were comprehensive. From this we can readily assume that U.S. intelligence monitored all such communications from the moment that KAL Flight 007 approached Kamchatka, and that NSA officials knew precisely what was happening when it happened—further evidence of which we shall note in a moment. Thirdly, it is also evident that the Soviets themselves have long been fully aware of this comprehensive monitoring of their air defense communications. Obviously, there can be no valid considerations of "national security" for continuing to conceal the fact and scope of such monitoring from the Soviets a quarter of a century later. And this raises questions about why, if they support the Reagan Administration's version of the KAL incident, the full transcripts of taped Soviet radio communications haven't been released—not even to the International Civil Aviation Organization team which investigated the incident.

Lastly, Bamford's account gives us a sense of the provocative and extremely dangerous nature of the intelligence game that the NSA has been playing for some three decades along the periphery of Russia's strategic regions—going so far, at times, as to deliberately penetrate Soviet airspace in order to activate, and monitor, Russia's air defense systems.

Indeed, these activities so alarmed two NSA analysts, Bernon F. Mitchell and William H. Martin, as to cause their defections to the Soviet Union in 1959. As Bamford tells the story,

> That America engaged in such dangerous and provocative activities shocked both Martin and Mitchell. While not averse to intelligence collection per se, they felt that by sending aircraft across borders and into hostile territory, the American government was foolishly risking igniting a spark that could set off World War III. Even worse was the fact that very few government officials appeared to be aware of the true nature of the missions. Senator Hubert Humphrey's attacks on the Soviet Union for its unprovoked actions against the EC-130 seemed to indicate that Congress also had been kept in the dark about the policy of border penetrations.[33]

Accordingly, Martin and Mitchell obtained an interview with Congressman Wayne Hays of Ohio, who had publicly raised the question of whether the State Department had given Congress a full account of the EC-130 incident. The two men tried to tell Hays about "the aircraft's true mission and their fears that such border crossings were a danger to world peace." Hays suggested that a Congressional investigation might be in order; but, suspecting that Martin and Mitchell had been sent by the CIA to test his ability to keep a secret, Hays dropped the issue. Martin and Mitchell, increasingly fearful and disillusioned, defected to the Soviet Union several months later. Although they soon became disillusioned with life in the Soviet Union as well, their story bears dramatic witness to the dangerous nature of the intelligence game the NSA has been playing, unknown to Congress and the general public, along the Soviet Union's periphery.[34]

It was against this background that KAL Flight 007 had "strayed" into the Sea of Okhotsk region, overflying two widely separated and highly sensitive Soviet strategic positions before it was shot down. It was also against this background that the Reagan Administration initially claimed that the United States possessed no "real time information" about the KAL airliner's deviant flight and that U.S. information about it had to be retrieved and translated from the Japanese.

The plausibility of the Reagan Administration's initial version of U.S. intelligence capabilities rested on public ignorance of the aggressive American intelligence efforts described by Bamford and the *New York Times.* In fact, American electronic intelligence stations engaged in around-the-clock surveillance are scattered all along the seas of Japan and Okhotsk. There is the Communications Security Group located at Wakkanai, on a peninsula which juts out from Hokkaido just to the southwest of La Perouse Strait. There is another electronic intelligence station at a 1229-acre base near Chitose, in southern Hokkaido. And there is still another one at Misawa Air Base, in northern Honshu, where 1,600 intelligence operators and analysts are engaged in the electronic monitoring operation.[35]

The obvious function of the station at Wakkanai is to monitor all Soviet military communications in the neighboring region and to track all aircraft; operators at the Wakkanai station, a mere forty miles from Sakhalin, could not have failed to monitor the radio communications between Soviet air controllers and the fighter pilots sent up to intercept the intruding aircraft as it approached southern Sakhalin. A transcript of the communications between the pilots, made public by the White House on September 6, showed that the Soviet fighter pilots stalked the aircraft for a full half hour (from 1756 to 1826 Greenwich mean time) before the missile was launched which brought the airliner down. The operators at Wakkanai doubtless followed their conversations from the very beginning—listening to, among other things, the Soviet pilot who shot Flight 007 down as he "locked on to the target" with weapon system "turned on" (1813). Moreover, such operators normally write "what they call a 'gist' for their superiors when they hear something considered alarming such as the conversations between the . . . pilots and their controllers. The gist usually triggers high-level attention and priority transcription by intelligence agencies of pertinent parts of the tape."[36]

Soviet interceptors closing in for the kill on an unidentified aircraft should have aroused urgent attention. It should also have produced immediate efforts to identify the aircraft through its IFF and/or one of the international emergency frequencies, and attempts to warn the aircraft that it was in danger. And yet, from all we know and can reasonably assume, the Wakkanai station followed the unfolding drama for at least half an hour—until the very moment Flight 007 was shot down—and did nothing. One can readily understand why Reagan Administration officials had pretended that the U.S. has no "real time" intelligence from the area, under the very nose of the Wakkanai electronic intelligence station, where the airliner met its demise. For knowledge of what was going on and a failure to warn the aircraft would strongly suggest that, although the aircraft was in extreme danger, the American intelligence authorities had reasons for not wanting to intervene. But what else, given the capabilities and functions of the Wakkanai electronic intelligence station, can we plausibly conclude?

Then, on September 4, senior Reagan Administration officials acknowledged that the Soviets had spotted an American RC-135 reconnaissance plane in the vicinity two hours before KAL Flight 007 was shot down and, as the *New York Times* reported, "apparently throught that both aircraft were American reconnaissance planes."[37] The *Washington Post* was more specific, quoting one such official as saying that the RC-135 flew "close to" Flight 007 "for a few minutes" in international waters off the Russian [Kamchatka] coast and at one point "crossed paths" with the airliner.[38]

This disclosure, the *Times* noted, "appeared to come almost by accident," as Administration officials sought to clarify Congressman Jim Wright's description of taped radio communications by two Soviet pilots during the eight minutes before Flight 007 was shot down, which President Reagan had earlier played for a group of Congressmen. It was also a serious indiscretion, since that would have put the RC-135 in Flight 007's immediate vicinity shortly before the airliner intruded into Soviet airspace over Kamchatka. Indeed, the acknowledgment that the RC-135 had flown "close to" the airliner for several minutes, at one point crossing its path, corroborated the account given by Marshal Ogarkov at his news conference five days later. According to Ogarkov, the RC-135 had been operating for about two hours off the Kamchatka coast when "another plane" was detected in the same area. ". . . those two planes rendezvoused and for some time, approximately ten minutes in that region, they were flying side by side. Then one of them could be observed, followed by the radios, turned back and flew to Alaska while the second plane went straight to Petropavlovsk in Kamchatka."[39]

The apparently inadvertent disclosure of the RC-135's presence in the same vicinity was followed by a series of explanations calculated to dissociate the RC-135 completely from the KAL airliner's venture into Soviet strategic airspace. Administration officials would insist at the outset that, whatever initial confusion there might have been, the two aircraft were a thousand miles apart by the time the airliner was shot down— and that the Soviets therefore had had plenty of time to establish the airliner's identity before they shot it down. The emphasis on where the RC-135 was when Flight 007 was shot down, and on what the Soviets may or may not have been able to establish about its identity, directed attention away from what the RC-135 was doing when the airliner was crossing Kamchatka. On that question, Administration officials would later assert that the RC-135 never came closer than 50 miles to the Kamchatka coast and never closer than 75 miles to the KAL airliner.[40] The earlier acknowledgement that the RC-135 had flown "close to" the airliner "for a few minutes," at one time crossing its path, was simply made to disappear.

But what motive could there have been for the original description of the proximity and actions of the two aircraft, had the official giving that account not understood it to be true? It is far more reasonable to assume that it was he who had been telling the truth, however indiscreetly. The fact that his account so closely paralleled that of Marshal Ogarkov lends further support to the conclusion that those matching accounts were both essentially correct.

Writing in *The Nation*, David Pearson has also made some careful calculations concerning the Korean airliner's location in relation to the orbit being flown by the RC-135. He notes that the airliner, which did not enter Soviet airspace until it was over Kamchatka, could not have flown to the east of the Soviet-owned Commander Islands—about a hundred miles off the Kamchtka coast. For it would then "have been approximately on course and it would have avoided Kamchatka entirely." It therefore had to have flown to the west of those islands. Given its flying speed of approximately 550 miles per hour, that would have put the airliner off the northeast coast of Kamchatka two and a half hours before it was shot down—at approximately the same time and place where U.S. officials acknowledged that the RC-135 had been orbiting off the Kamchatka coast.[41]

Could the RC-135, in such circumstances, have been unaware that the Korean airliner had soon afterwards intruded into Soviet airspace, arousing the attentions of Soviet air defenses on Kamchatka? Information about the capabilities and functions of RC-135s, which carry both radar and electronic surveillance equipment, soon appeared in the Western press; and these accounts were extremely enlightening. As the *New York Times* reported, "The primary mission of the RC-135 fleet," operating from airfields along Russia's perimeter, "is to track Soviet air-defense activity and missile tests." The aircraft, operated for the National Security Agency by the Air Force, "collect information about the abilities of Soviet radar systems, monitor communications between Soviet jet fighter pilots and ground controllers and observe the final stages of test flights of Soviet intercontinental ballistic missile flights."[42]

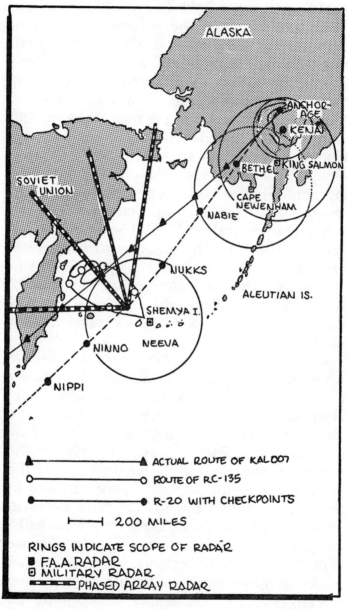

Map: Paul Gordon   Source: David Pearson, *The Nation*

Military sources told George Wilson of the *Washington Post* that the particular RC-135 in question had been "on an intelligence mission to assess Soviet air defenses." And they provided this picture of what was going on—most certainly as the Korean airliner was overflying Kamchatka: "Air Force technicians in the rear of the RC-135 were listening to and recording Soviet voice and electronic communications as they lumbered along in the military version of the Boeing 707 airliner." Those same military sources also told Wilson that it was standard practice for American military aircraft to "tickle" Soviet radar into action. "They said this amounts to flying close enough to air defenses to cause the Soviets to activate search radar and perhaps fire-control radar and to talk about what they are seeing and doing in response to the unidentified aircraft overhead."[43]

In this case it had not been a military aircraft which had "tickled" Soviet air defenses into action; it had been the KAL airliner which had "accidentally" overflown Kamchatka, activating the air defense systems which protect the giant Russian naval base at Petropavlovsk—this for the benefit of the electronic eavesdroppers in the RC-135 which "fortuitously" happened to be in the vicinity. Could the RC-135 have failed to track the KAL airliner's flight over Kamchatka and to monitor the Soviet response? "Intelligence experts out of the Government" pointed to what was entirely evident: ". . . if the surveillance plane was anywhere near the path of the South Korean plane during the early phases of its encounter with Soviet aircraft, the American plane would likely have detected unusual Soviet air-defense activity. If so, they said, the crew of the plane could have taken steps to notify civilian air-traffic controllers in Japan."[44]

Then, on September 13, Tom Bernard and T. Edward Eskelson, both former Air Force communications specialists who had flown on RC-135 flights out of Okinawa, provided a detailed description of RC-135 capabilities in the *Denver Post*. Among other things, they noted that even if the particular RC-135 in question had returned to its base there would have been another such aircraft off the Kamchatka coast to replace it:

> The aircraft is deemed so important to overall U.S. intelligence collection efforts in sensitive, high-priority target areas that it is always relieved on its orbit by yet another RC-135 just prior to the conclusion of its mission. This procedure allows for routine, 24-hour-a-day, 365-day-a-year intercept coverage of sensitive and important target areas. We find the inference made by President Reagan that the Sakhalin-Kamchatka target area was abandoned by the RC-135 intercept platform to be unbelievable and contrary to NSA policy.[45]

From all this, we can see why the Reagan Administration had publicly sought to put as much distance as possible between the RC-135 and KAL Flight 007. For public knowledge that an RC-135 had been nearby when the airliner overflew Kamchatka, and knowledge of the RC-135's capabilities, would raise extremely embarrassing—even dangerous—questions: What might have been the connection between the RC-

135 and the airliner's flight into Soviet airspace? How could an aircraft with the RC-135's capabilities not have monitored everything that was going on, with the highly sophisticated equipment it carried, and why was no attempt made to warn Japanese air traffic controllers, the airliner itself, or even Soviet authorities?

Meanwhile, with information about U.S. intelligence capabilities beginning to surface in the press, the Reagan Administration plainly found it impossible to continue pretending that it had been obliged to reconstruct what happened to Flight 007 from Japanese and Korean sources, hours after the event. On September 13, the same day the Bernard-Eskelson article appeared in the *Denver Post*, "senior intelligence officials" acknowledged that, "The existence of independent American information about the attack had been shielded to protect United States intelligence sources and methods." The intelligence officials said that "highly sensitive United States monitoring equipment detected a sudden increase in Soviet air-defense activity over the Kamchatka Peninsula and the Sea of Okhotsk in the early morning hours of September 1. The activity included stepped-up radar surveillance followed by the dispatch of several interceptor aircraft, according to officials."[46] At one point, according to these officials, a Soviet surface-to-air missile unit was ordered to track a target identified as an RC-135 reconnaissance plane— but little was made of this on the American side because the only RC-135 in the area was headed back for its base.

But in this new version of the American role, the "highly sensitive" monitoring equipment did not include anything which would have detected a Boeing 747 as it flew over Kamchatka and the NSA technicians were unable to discover from their monitoring of Soviet communications that the Soviet jet fighters had scrambled to intercept an intruding aircraft. As one U.S. intelligence official put it, the technicians monitoring this unusual Soviet air defense activity "had no way of knowing at the time that a commercial airliner had entered Soviet airspace and was the object of the maneuvers." The technicians purportedly concluded, therefore, that these unusual Soviet actions were part of an air defense exercise.

Moreover, these intelligence officials asserted that even if the necessary information had been acquired in time to warn the KAL airliner, it would have been difficult to do so. Said one "senior" official: "There's no system of merging the day-to-day work of the intelligence community with the day-to-day work of the airline control people." Other officials added that NSA's heavy emphasis on security would make its officials hesitant, in the absence of a clear emergency, to share information with anyone outside the intelligence community.[47]

In this explanation, the RC-135 which had been patrolling off the Kamchatka coast near the point where Flight 007 intruded into Soviet airspace had simply been made to disappear—to be replaced by "highly sensitive United States monitoring equipment" at some unspecified location. And that enabled the intelligence officials in question to construct a story whereby the intelligence operators monitoring Soviet air defense activity over Kamchatka ostensibly would not have known that the object of Soviet attentions was the KAL airliner.

But this explanation was quite as implausible as the original story put out by Richard Burt. If Soviet air defense systems on Kamchatka were being adequately monitored by other U.S. electronic intelligence facilities, would there have been around-the-clock RC-135 patrolling off the Kamchatka coast? Surely not. And can it be doubted that this monitoring of Soviet air defense activity over Kamchatka, while the KAL airliner flew overhead, had in fact been carried out by the RC-135 which had been patrolling nearby for the specific purpose of assessing Soviet air defenses?

Picture, for a moment, this scene. The RC-135 patrols in the vicinity of Flight 007—in all likelihood flying close to it for several minutes, as both Marshal Ogarkov and an unidentified Reagan Administration official said it had. The airliner then heads for the Kamchatka coast. And the RC-135, with radar enabling it to "track Soviet air-defense activity and missile tests," would certainly have tracked the airliner as it flew in that direction. Then the RC-135's intelligence operators would have heard Soviet air controllers attempting to contact an intruding aircraft on 121 megacycles, an international emergency frequency, doubtless attempting to identify the aircraft on IFF as well—but without eliciting any response. Very soon thereafter, those operators would have heard radio communications with the Soviet fighter pilots as they scrambled to intercept the intruder. Are we really to believe that U.S. intelligence operators, following the entire sequence of events, were unable to discover that this wasn't an "air defense exercise"? Would anyone reading this book, had he or she been on the RC-135, have failed to put two and two together, concluding that it was the airliner which had been responsible for activating Soviet air defenses on Kamchatka?

Moreover, after the Soviet interceptors scrambled into the air over Kamchatka, the Soviets, by their account as well as Washington's, tracked the intruding aircraft as it flew towards southern Sakhalin. There would certainly have been continuing radio communications between air defense officials on Kamchatka and higher Soviet authorities concerning the identity and flight path of the aircraft which had overflown Kamchatka. Indeed, a U.S. intelligence source told George Wilson of the *Washington Post* that, "the Soviet controllers followed their practice of radioing information about intruders from the border air bases up the chain of command as far as Moscow, giving U.S. and Japanese eavesdroppers several chances to record the messages."[48] Yet, for well over an hour and a half after the KAL airliner had overflown Kamchatka, U.S. intelligence officials continued to watch and listen in silence as the airliner headed for the highly sensitive, and strongly defended, Soviet positions at the tip of southern Sakhalin.

What explains this silence? It is hard to take

seriously the contention that the absence of a system "merging" the day-to-day work of the intelligence community with that of "the airline control people" precluded a warning to Japanese air control stations. Since there are large numbers of civilian, military, and intelligence aircraft operating in the region (not to speak of Soviet aircraft), there necessarily have to be established procedures for communications between military/intelligence facilities and civilian ground control—even if day-to-day operations aren't "merged." And there are doubtless occasions on which these channels are routinely used.

In fact, the RC-135 itself, as Bernard and Eskelson noted, "has the capability of transmitting messages over an extremely broad range of radio frequencies, including those used by other aircraft, both civilian and military, ships, ground stations and *air controllers* [emphasis added]." Quite evidently, U.S. intelligence not only knew what was happening, but had ready means for warning both the KAL airliner and Japanese ground controllers. They issued no such warning.

Where does all this leave us? We have already seen that Japanese air controllers had every reason to become alarmed when Flight 007, having given a grossly inaccurate position, did not appear on their radar screens—but did nothing. And we have seen that American intelligence operators at Wakkanai (and perhaps elsewhere) doubtless monitored the communications of Soviet interceptor pilots as they stalked and then closed in on the KAL airliner over Sakhalin—

and failed to warn the airliner. And now, we have every reason to believe that U.S. intelligence knew what was happening from the moment Flight 007 approached Kamchatka—and this produced no warning either. Why did no one warn the airliner? There has to be an explanation, and we are increasingly entitled to suspect that it can't be admitted to "for security reasons."

5. HOW DID FLIGHT 007 ELUDE SOVIET AIR DEFENSES OVER KAMCHATKA?

Still another question: how did Flight 007 manage to fly across Kamchatka, a Soviet strategic territory with substantial air defenses, before it could be headed off? This would not be an easy task for an airliner which just happened to stray in that direction. The Soviets doubtless routinely track all aircraft flying anywhere near the Kamchatka coast and would observe any aircraft heading toward Kamchatka; it could be anticipated that they would attempt to intercept any such aircraft. Nonetheless, KAL Flight 007 managed to overfly Kamchatka and almost to exit from Soviet airspace before Soviet interceptors were able to get anywhere near it. Conceivably, this could be attributed in part to a poor state of Soviet readiness and/or uncertainty about the intruding plane's identity. But there is also evidence to suggest that pre-planned evasive maneuvers by the pilot, and perhaps external help, also played a role.

We have already noted that Flight 007 evidently maintained radio silence as it flew across

Kamchatka and also had its IFF system turned off. The Soviets have also charged that Flight 007 was flying without lights—a charge the Reagan Administration strove to refute by playing a tape on which the Soviet pilot who shot the airliner down is heard to say, "The A.N.O. [air navigation lights] are burning. The [strobe] light is flashing."[49] But what this refers to isn't clear. That statement followed by a few seconds the fighter pilot's report to Soviet ground control that he was "executing" ground control's instruction. The Soviet pilot could have been referring to the intruding aircraft—or to the fact that he had started to flash his own lights, an established procedure under international aviation rules for warning a straying aircraft at night. Indeed, it is logical that he would have done this. Only two minutes later, the Soviet pilot reported that he had "broken off lock-on" and was "firing cannon bursts"—suggesting that the intruding aircraft had ignored earlier warnings.

Whatever the case, it is also very possible that Flight 007 was flying without lights *during the first stage* of its two-stage flight over Soviet strategic territories. A Russian fighter pilot sent up to intercept the intruding aircraft over Kamchatka would state, in a Soviet television interview: "Even on the side of the dark area of the sky there were no signs of any illumination on the aircraft."[50] It is hard to imagine that Soviet jet fighters would have had any difficulties in intercepting the airliner had it been flying with its air navigation lights on and its strobe light flashing.

It is also in this context that the RC-135 intelligence plane comes into the picture again. While asserting that the RC-135 was simply on a "routine mission," a senior Administration official acknowledged that its presence in the area might have caused the Soviets to have been confused initially—mistaking the airliner for the RC-135.[51] Had that confusing presence, like so many other elements in this tragic affair, also been sheer happenstance?

The Soviets have charged that it wasn't. At his September 9 news conference, Marshal Ogarkov pointed to a large chart purportedly showing the flight paths of the two aircraft and affirmed that the RC-135 "obviously played the control in the . . . initial phase." Also, ". . . as we can see on this flight chart . . . their flights were certainly coordinated so as to make our task more difficult and confused our Air Defense Forces."[52] Four days later the Soviet Defense Ministry newspaper, *Krasnaya Zvezda,* further claimed that the RC-135 had dived below Soviet radar cover off Kamchatka "to distract air-defense crews and enable the 747 to enter Soviet airspace undetected."[53] It happens to be the case, as Bernard and Eskelson noted, that RC-135s carry equipment designed "to 'jam' radar and radio transmissions in addition to certain electronic systems in other aircraft. This capability was used in Vietnam to 'confuse' Soviet supplied air defense radars and aircraft."[54] Was it also used to help Flight 007 overfly Kamchatka? It seems unlikely that a commercial airliner would have been able to so easily penetrate Soviet airspace without evasive maneuvers and the admittedly "confusing" presence of the RC-135.

Had the U.S. reconnaissance plane's confusing presence been by intent, as the Soviets charged, the Reagan Administration obviously could not have been expected to admit it—for that would clearly show that Flight 007 was on a mission abetted, and presumably instigated, by the United States. Yet what we see here is still another element of "sheer happenstance" which combined "fortuitously" with a series of "errors," "equipment failures," "inadequate procedures," and "pure accident" to make possible the KAL airliner's uninterrupted flight across Kamchatka and the Sea of Okhotsk—on a course which would take it precisely over a highly sensitive Soviet strategic base at the tip of southern Sakhalin.

In sum, the Reagan Administration's explanations for how KAL Flight 007 happened to "stray off course" and get shot down 2½ hours later rest on a whole series of extremely implausible circumstances. If the Administration's explanations for even one of these circumstances were invalid, the entire case for an "accidental flight" would come crashing down. Yet the odds against all of these virtually inconceivable errors of commission and omission taking place as described are astronomical. The logical and factual absurdities in the Reagan Administration's account suggest that we have been presented with a cover story.

6. THE INTERNATIONAL CIVIL AVIATION ORGANIZATION'S FINDINGS

We are not done yet, however, with hypotheses about how Flight 007 might have "accidentally strayed" across the entire Sea of Okhotsk region. The International Civil Aviation Organization (ICAO), a United Nations affiliate, conducted an investigation of the KAL airliner incident; and in early December 1983, the investigating team submitted its report to the ICAO's governing Council. The report reached two basic conclusions: (1) It rejected the Soviet argument that, in the ICAO's words, there had been " a premeditated deviation from the flight plan route for intelligence purposes." (2) It concluded that crew error had been responsible for deviation from Flight 007's planned route—that deviation beginning "soon after its departure from Anchorage." The ICAO, in fixing upon the "crew error" explanation, had rejected as "too unlikely to warrant further investigation" the possibilities of extensive navigation systems failures, deliberate crew action to save fuel, crew incapacitation, and unlawful interference.[55] Thus, having ruled out all possibilities save one, the ICAO investigating team had set out to discover, mainly through computer simulations, how Flight 007 might have ended up where it did—and assumed that the necessary "crew errors" had in fact taken place.

Yet the ICAO team's findings also seem heavily flawed. Let us consider those findings and how they were arrived at. The ICAO "Summary of Findings and Conclusions" states that, "Soon after its departure from Anchorage, KE007 began deviating to the right (north) of its assigned direct route to Bethel [the first way point]." This, according to the report, produced a "progressively ever greater lateral displacement to the right of its planned route"—with the aircraft continuing on its mistaken course "for some five hours and twenty-six minutes" until it was shot down after overflying both Kamchatka and Sakhalin. Furthermore, despite the length of that digression, "No evidence was found . . . to indicate that the flight crew of KE007 was, at any time, aware of the flight's deviation from its planned route . . ."[56]

It is not difficult to see how the investigating team's basic thesis was arrived at. If the aircraft's inertial navigation system (INS) had been properly programmed, and was functioning, Flight 007's gross deviation from its assigned route would not have been possible. And if one were to rule out a deliberate veering away from its assigned route, some time after the aircraft left Anchorage, one would then *have to* assume that crew error had caused the aircraft to head off in the wrong direction from the very outset—taking it quite by chance, out of all the possibilities for random error, over the Soviet strategic positions which it overflew.

How, then, did Flight 007's crew head off in the wrong direction "virtually from the beginning of its ill-fated flight"? And how could they have "navigated" their aircraft for five and a half hours—from Anchorage, across Alaska and the North Pacific, then across Kamchatka and the Sea of Okhotsk, up to the very moment when the aircraft was shot down after overflying Sakhalin, without ever realizing that anything was amiss? The ICAO's "key findings" about this did not derive from the "limited hard evidence available to the investigators." Rather, those findings derived from "postulated and then simulated, most-likely scenarios of what may have transpired." The simulations, carried out for the ICAO by the Boeing Aircraft Corporation (a major U.S. military contractor), finally produced two scenarios deemed "possible explanations" for Flight 007's deviation from its assigned route. Those scenarios were:

(1) That the crew inadvertently flew virtually the entire flight on a constant magnetic heading (in the "heading mode") due to its unawareness of the fact that "heading" had been selected as the mode of navigation rather than "inertial navigation system" (INS) . . .

(2) That an undetected 10 degree longitudinal error was made in inserting the "present position" coordinates of the Anchorage gate position into one or more of the INS (inertial navigation system) units on board the aircraft.

The report acknowledged that each scenario "assumes a considerable degree of lack of alertness and attentiveness on the part of the entire flight crew," but affirmed that this would not have been "to a degree that is unknown in international civil aviation circles."

How plausible are these scenarios? Speaking about the "crew error" hypothesis shortly after the Korean airliner had been shot down, the operations director of an airline which regularly flies Flight 007's prescribed route was incredulous. "He said," according to the *San Francisco Examiner and Chronicle,* "that for the Korean airliner to have ended up where it did, its crew would have had to have made at least 10 separate errors in programming the inertial navigation system." The official added that, "The error was so gross it almost seems deliberate."[57]

The manner in which the INS system is programmed was described in the same article:

> The INS is programmed by keying into a digital keyboard a set of latitude and longitude figures representing reporting points on the jet routes. The keyboard resembles the buttons of a Touch-tone telephone . . .
> Pilots say that the usual U.S. airline practice is to program each INS separately, although it is possible to program only one and use that as a master to program the backup computers.[58]

The ICAO report described the way in which Flight 007's crew was presumed to have entered a 10 degree longitudinal error in the airliner's INS computers, causing those computers to assume that Anchorage was 300 miles east (139° 58′) of its actual position (149° 58′) when the aircraft took off: "Such an entry mistake could be made by a single 'finger error' in entering more than

100 digits and letters that would be needed to fully load a single INS unit at the outset of the flight."

As everyone knows, "finger errors" are easy to commit—whether one is making a telephone call, typing on a typewriter, or programming a computer. But we are speaking here of a navigation system of such sophistication that it was used to guide Apollo astronauts to the moon—with "gyroscopes and accelerometers . . . so sensitive and reliable they can bring an airliner to within a mile or two of its destination in a trans-Pacific flight."[59] Common sense tells us that routine, highly reliable procedures would have been designed to insure that the INS is programmed correctly. Otherwise, finger errors could be expected to negate the value of this otherwise extremely well designed system, sending airliners all over the place.

Hence the remarks of Captain William Powers, a Pan Am pilot who flies the New York-Anchorage-Tokyo route:

> After the data has been entered, it is checked by another member of the flight crew using printed navigational charts to confirm each set of coordinates. This procedure is crucial. If the wrong numbers are entered, the plane will fly to the wrong place. That is why double-checking is important.[60]

Similarly, the *San Francisco Examiner* noted that, "Standard pre-takeoff procedures . . . call for the crew to direct the computers to run through the flight theoretically, using the figures just fed into them. If some of the figures are wrong, the computers will show the aircraft ending up in the wrong place."[61] Since the possibility for a "finger error" is always there, it would be virtually unthinkable not to carry out such checking procedures. Yet that is what the ICAO investigating team presumes the KAL airliner's highly experienced crew to have done.

Even if an INS programming error had gone undetected, noted the *Examiner*, "there are so many other navigational checks in crossing the Pacific that a vast error seems virtually impossible unless the South Korean crew was asleep."[62] To begin with, the crew would also have had to have botched the first leg of its flight—over land, from Anchorage to the Bethel way point. "Over land," as Richard Witkin noted, "the primary navigation system is a network of VOR (very high frequency omnidirectional radio) stations. A crew tunes to a station's frequency. An instrument shows the direction to that station and keeps clicking off the number of miles to it."[63] It is when an aircraft is over the ocean, out of range of VOR stations, that navigation becomes dependent primarily upon the INS. Thus, however Flight 007's INS might have been programmed, its VOR receiver would have told its crew precisely what the aircraft's heading was in relation to the Bethel VOR station during the entire length of its flight from Anchorage to Bethel. If the aircraft had deviated from its prescribed course, the pilot would have perceived it quickly.

Moreover, had the INS been wrongly programmed in the manner postulated by the ICAO investigating team, the Anchorage to Bethel distance recorded in the computer's memory would have been 650 miles—whereas the actual distance is 350 miles. Flight 007's crew had flown R20 many times and after about 40 minutes would have expected both the VOR receiver and the inertial display to show the aircraft to be reaching Bethel. If the aircraft had deviated in the manner postulated by the ICAO, it would have flown distinctly north of Bethel. The VOR needle would have veered towards the south at an increasingly sharp angle as the aircraft came even with Bethel, showing its deviation in an increasingly unmistakeable manner; and at Bethel the needle would have swung from fore to aft. Yet, if the INS had been wrongly programmed, the "from" and "to" windows of the inertial display would have continued to show the Bethel way point to be still ahead.[64] Thus, Flight 007's crew could not have failed to notice that their aircraft was off course and that their INS was giving peculiar readings unless, again, they were sound asleep—waking up just long enough, one might suppose, to report to Anchorage air traffic controllers at precisely the right moment that they were in fact at Bethel.

There is another powerful VOR transmitter at Shemya, near the western extremity of the Aleutian chain, and it would have been been a normal procedure to tune into the Shemya station as the aircraft approached the Neeva waypoint. Had Flight 007's pilot tuned into Shemya, he would again have been able, as we have already noted, to ascertain his aircraft's direction and distance from that station—and also would have been able to determine whether or not there was agreement with the aircraft's position as shown by its INS.

Thus, whether Flight 007's crew was imagined to have wrongly programmed their INS or to be inadvertently flying on a "heading mode" (without noticing for the entire flight that the switch in the center of the cockpit panel was turned to that mode) they had means for precisely ascertaining their position at the Bethel and Neeva waypoints. We know that they reported at all the mandatory reporting points. Would they have reported that they were at Bethel, and then at Neeva, without bothering to use their VOR to ascertain where they in fact were? Why, under normal circumstances, would they not have followed this routine navigational procedure?

Witkin, Rudolph Braunberg, and the *Examiner* all pointed to another common navigational procedure—that of switching the aircraft's weather radar to "ground echo," enabling the pilot to see coastlines up to 200 miles away. "Since pilots are . . . aware of the dangers of straying over the Soviet Kurile Islands," reported the *Examiner,* "they also usually use their weather radar in its terrain-mapping mode even in clear weather to keep clear of the islands"—and doubtless clear of Kamchatka as well.[65] Braunberg, a former Lufthansa Airlines pilot, also noted that there are several radio beacons on Kamchatka—at Kubaru, Kokutan, and Lopatka—"whose bearings can be taken by using good old radio compass navigation."[66] We know that Flight 007's pilot at one point told Tokyo air controllers that he was 113 miles southeast of Hokkaido and that, "We passed safely south of Kamchatka." How could he have known these things unless he had used his instruments to determine where he was? And how could he not have discovered that he wasn't anywhere near where he said he was if he had used his instruments to determine his position?

Consider, finally, this Associated Press report of "What It's Like in a Cockpit on the North Pacific Route." The Pan Am crew, after entering the coordinates in their INS computer, confirming the accuracy of each set of coordinates, and taking off, continued to check their position throughout the flight.

> Ten minutes before each checkpoint was reached, coordinates stored in the computer for the next checkpoint were verified by the crew, by calling up the data from the computer and comparing it with printed charts.
>
> Ten minutes after each checkpoint and position report, the crew checked its position again on the computer and plotted it on a navigational chart. Between checkpoints, instruments were constantly monitored to insure that the plane was on course and at the right speed and altitude.[67]

The navigation of an aircraft across the North Pacific is clearly an active process, wherein the pilot and crew follow specific routine procedures at various points to insure that their navigational instruments are properly programmed and/or functioning, and to insure that they are on course. One does not simply program the INS in a casual manner, take off from the Anchorage airport, and retire from the cockpit on the assumption that the aircraft will automatically arrive, after seven hours or so, at the Tokyo airport. Yet that, in essence, is what the ICAO investigating team assumed Flight 007's crew to have done. It assumed that the airliner's crew did not properly carry out any of a whole series of routine procedures—any *one* of which, properly carried out, would have negated the possibility of a gross deviation in the first instance or enabled the crew to discover that deviation and bring the aircraft back on course. The picture here is of an unbelievably incompetent, irresponsible, and careless air crew.

On a computer simulation, perhaps anything is conceivable. But was it conceivable in the real world, given all the procedures a pilot normally follows to navigate his aircraft to its destination? Had fate somehow assigned to KAL Flight 007 just the kind of pilot who might have botched the entire five-and-a-half hour flight in all the ways required to sustain the ICAO's computer-produced explanation? This is how *People* magazine described Flight 007's pilot in its December 26, 1983 issue:

> Korean Air Lines pilot Chun Byung In, 45, was, by all accounts, compulsively orderly. Immaculately dressed in his freshly pressed blue uniform, two neatly ironed handkerchiefs folded in his pockets, the onetime Korean air force stunt pilot cut an imposing figure on the international civilian flights he had commanded flawlessly for 11 years. "You never saw such a methodical man as my husband," says his widow, Kim Ok Hee. "Just about everything had to be precisely at its proper place."

Ahn Sang Jeon, who had flown precisely synchronized formations with Chun on the South Korean Air Force's aerobatics team, described Chun as "the most careful man I've ever known." He was so respected, observed *People*, "that he had served as a backup captain on three of President Chun Doo Hwan's state visits . . ." And this was the man who had committed one gross navigational error after another in piloting Flight 007 on its deviant course? To ask that question, it seems to me, is to answer it.

We can nonetheless see why an almost unbelievably careless and incompetent crew had to have been postulated by the ICAO's investigating team: without such a crew the only explanations for Flight 007's flight over Soviet strategic territories the investigators could imagine, or accept, would have to have been rejected. But the scenarios postulated by the ICAO investigating team were so implausible that the organization's own expert review panel, the Air Navigation Commission, stated that it could not validate any of them. All those scenarios, said the commission, "contained some points which could not be explained satisfactorily."[68]

If KAL Flight 007's lengthy excursion across Soviet strategic territories had not been accidental, it would have to have been intentional. The ICAO report stated that they found no evidence of this. Quite obviously, Flight 007's crew would not have *reported* an uncorrected deviation of the kind their aircraft carried out, had they been aware of it; for it obviously would have been both intentional and highly irregular, to say the least. Yet, as we have seen, there had indeed been aspects of Flight 007's behavior which raised troubling questions: its failure to respond to another KAL airliner's attempt to make routine radio contact; its unresponsiveness to attempts doubtless made by the Soviets to contact it on an international emergency frequency; the fact that its IFF had evidently been turned off; its ignoring of warnings by Soviet interceptors over Sakhalin. Questions about these and other aspects of the airliner's behavior had been raised in the Western press. They were important questions, and they all suggested intent. But the ICAO report avoids facing such questions.

The ICAO report was also seriously deficient in other respects. The failure of U.S. and Japanese air traffic controllers (not to speak of U.S. intelligence) to warn Flight 007 that it was off course was a proper and plainly important subject of investigation. But here the ICAO investigators ran into a stone wall. Of the evidence bearing on the role of air traffic controllers and U.S. intelligence, the ICAO "Summary of Findings and Conclusions" says only that the ICAO "was not provided any radar recordings, recorded communications or transcripts associated with the first intercept attempt or for the ground-to-interceptor portion of the second attempt . . ." In other words, they didn't get anything which hadn't already been given to the newspapers. Apparently, the ICAO had asked for additional transcripts and recordings but their requests had been denied. Yves Lambert, the organization's Secretary General, reported at a meeting of its council that information had been withheld by the U.S., Japanese and Soviet governments—an extraordinary circumstance, since the ICAO had made its requests in the context of an investigation into the causes of a disaster which brought death to 246 airline passengers.

One result, of course, was to keep the entire blame for the tragedy on the Soviet Union—where the U.S. Government clearly wanted it to stay. A second result was to keep the ICAO itself committed to the wholly implausible explanation for Flight 007's deviation from its assigned course which the ICAO investigators had put forward.

In conclusion, what is clear about the ICAO's entire "investigative" procedure is that they almost entirely ignored the multitude of circumstances surrounding the airliner's flight which raised troubling questions about its own behavior and that of air controllers and intelligence operators who should have detected and warned the airliner, but didn't do so; also, that the ICAO's investigating team (though not its expert review panel) had ignored everything which might have raised questions about the "inattentive crew" theory required by its computer-simulated scenarios. As an old Chinese saying goes, they had plainly "cut the foot to fit the shoe."

Least of all had the ICAO investigating team been disposed to follow up leads which suggested that Flight 007 might have been on a U.S. intelligence mission. The ICAO dealt with this question by noting that the airliner had left Anchorage at its scheduled departure time, which would have resulted in an "on-time" arrival at Seoul. In light of this, said the report, "the investigation did not consider further the hypothesis considered by the USSR Accident Investigation Commission that there was a deliberate delay in KE007's departure from Anchorage and a premeditated deviation from the flight plan route for intelligence gathering purposes." So that, as they saw it, took care of that potentially explosive question. But what they had done was to erect a straw man which could easily be knocked down. The question of whether or not Flight 007 had been on an intelligence mission rested very little on the possibility of a delayed departure. There were, in fact, many suspicious tracks in the terrain ostensibly examined by the ICAO investigators—tracks which those investigators plainly chose "not to see" or to follow.

Where, then, does all this leave us? We have examined the explanations given by both the Reagan Administration and the ICAO's investigating team, and have found, I think, that they are inconsistent with too many technical factors, too many actions we could reasonably expect from all the actors in the affair, and too many other circumstances. Yet there must be an explanation for the tragedy over which much of the nation was stirred to self-righteous wrath; the circumstances surrounding the flight have to add up to something. Let us now consider what that explanation might in fact be—and what, indeed, might be the true significance of Flight 007's ill-fated passage over Kamchatka and Sakhalin.

PART TWO: THE CONTEXT

7. THE STRATEGIC CONTEXT FOR THE KAL AIRLINER'S FLIGHT

The apparently "inexplicable" nature of the entire affair derives partly from the fact that, in the accounts given of it, the downing of the KAL airliner had been abstracted from any strategic or historical context. The emphasis has been placed almost entirely on the last moments of the affair, when the Soviets shot the airliner down. Thus, the only *meaning* ascribed to this otherwise "purely accidental" event was that it provided still another example of Soviet "brutality" and "paranoia"—contrasted, of course, to the "concern for human life" demonstrated by the Reagan Administration's expressions of sympathy for the victims.

But it all begins to make sense when one considers the evolving strategic context in which this seemingly "accidental" event took place. As we have already noted, the Reagan Administration has been accelerating the American effort to develop capabilities for "fighting and winning" a nuclear war. More particularly, as a *New York Times* report by Richard Halloran revealed, the Reagan Administration's "1984–1988 Defense Guidance" called for development of the nuclear weapon systems required to carry out a strategy aimed at "decapitating" the Soviet state. It also called for the development of U.S. capabilities to "prevail" even in a "protracted" nuclear war.[69]

For Pentagon strategists to imagine that any such strategies could be "successful," the U.S. would have to be able to destroy Russia's command and control centers and its retaliatory capabilities before they could be brought into operation. This is precisely what the new weapon systems scheduled for deployment, or being pushed through Congress, are designed for. The highly accurate Pershing II missiles being deployed in West Germany are positioned no more than 6–8 minutes away from Soviet command and control centers in Western Russia. The MX missile, if and when deployed, would presumably be capable of destroying Soviet land-based missiles in their silos with a second-generation maneuvering warhead (MARV) designed to strike within 90 feet of its target. The Trident II missile, using a similar warhead, will be able to strike at Soviet land-based missiles from positions only ten minutes away.

This would leave only Russia's submarine-based missile force as a significant factor to be dealt with. In this regard, a Library of Congress report noted that, "If the United States achieves a disarming first-strike capability against Soviet ICBMs, and also develops an ASW (anti-submarine warfare) capability that, together with attacks on naval facilities, could practically negate the Soviet SSBN [ballistic missile-launching submarine] force, then the strategic balance as it has become to be broadly defined and accepted would no longer be stable."[70] It would no longer be stable because the United States would presumably then have an unanswerable capability for destroying Russia's nuclear forces with a first-strike attack; the Soviets, knowing this, would be given a strong incentive for launching a preemptive first strike during a grave international crisis; and the United States, knowing *this*, would have a strong incentive for attempting to beat the Soviets to the punch with its own preemptive first strike. As Paul Warnke and others have noted, humanity's survival, in a time of international crisis, would come to rest on a "hair trigger."

It was in this context that the U.S. Defense Advanced Research Projects Agency (DARPA) in 1975 launched Project Seaguard—designed to give the United States an integrated computerized system of capabilities for pinpointing and destroying all of the Soviet Union's missile-launching submarines.[71] The Soviets, certainly well apprised of the growing threat they are being presented with, are doubtless working as hard as they can to preserve the integrity of their deterrent systems and especially to strengthen the capabilities of their submarine-launched missile force—even as the Pentagon is working as hard as *it* can to perfect its capabilities for destroying Russia's submarines before they can be brought into operation.

The Soviet Union, with very little access to the oceans, operates under severe disadvantages in deploying its missile-launching submarines. There are only two points from which they can be deployed: from Murmansk, into the North Atlantic; and from bases on Russia's North Pacific coast. Until now the Soviet land-based missile force has been reasonably secure from attack, and the Soviets, in these circumstances, have kept approximately 85% of their submarines in port at all times. Moreover, their submarines at sea have been stalked incessantly with increasingly sophisticated electronic devices—airborne, seaborne, and under the sea. Those who have seen the BBC film, "Nuclear Nightmares," will remember vivid footage of Norwegian, British, and then American ASW aircraft stalking Soviet submarines from the moment they leave Murmansk, and the string of underwater sensors which have been laid to pick up their sounds.

The Soviets, for their part, have recently been reported to be deploying more submarines at sea—in the Mediterranean and Caribbean Seas as well as the Atlantic, Pacific, and Indian Oceans.[72] Moreover, the first of Russia's new, nuclear-powered Typhoon submarines became operational in December 1983, with eleven more to be built. The 25,000-ton Typhoon, easily the largest in the world, is equipped to carry 80 nuclear warheads on its 20 missiles—as against the 160 warheads carried by each of America's 31 Poseidon submarines or the minimum of 240 warheads carried by a U.S. Trident.

Unlike the second-generation Trident II missiles, to be installed on Trident submarines in 1989, the nuclear warheads carried by the Typhoon do not have the accuracy required for a first strike against land-based missiles in hardened silos. Yet the Typhoon's missiles have great range and pose a formidable *retaliatory* threat. Writing on "The Silent Chase," Thomas B. Allen and Norman Polmar noted that the Typhoon has also been designed to operate in a manner calculated to avoid detection and destruction:

> For an American attack submarine, the greatest challenge may be the new Soviet Typhoon-class missile submarine, operating beneath the Arctic ice pack. The Typhoon is well hidden from the eyes of antisubmarine surface ships and aircraft, and presents a difficult target for attack submarines as well. Sonar beams scanning the waters beneath the icecap, for example, have trouble distinguishing a hovering missile sub from the ice stalactites around it.[73]

Reportedly, the Soviet Typhoon fleet will operate from a secret new base in the Kurile Islands.

It is also in the context of the Pentagon's accelerated efforts to perfect its anti-submarine warfare capabilities that Soviet submarines have recently been discovered sneaking into Swedish coastal waters—a Swedish parliamentary report asserting that such violations took place at least 40 times in 1982. "One Swedish Defense Department theory," reported *New York Times* columnist Flora Lewis, "is that the Russians are practicing hiding in their neutral, well-mapped waters in the event of war."[74] The protection offered by Sweden's coastal waters is not simply because they are neutral. Allen and Polmar quoted a retired U.S. admiral, "a world authority on military electronics," as saying: "You'd be lucky to get 50-

yard detections even with 20,000-yard sonars in those waters. The salinity, low temperature, and shallow, irregular sea floor—it all works for the submariner. It's a beautiful place to hide submarines."[75] These Soviet forays into Swedish waters are of course illegal and have been counterproductive politically; but for the Soviets, the military stakes in trying to preserve the integrity of their submarine-based deterrent force could hardly be higher.

The region into which Flight 007 flew is the other side of this same strategic picture. There are four Soviet naval bases there. The headquarters for the Soviet Pacific Fleet is at Vladivostok. Also on the mainland, at Sovetskaya Gavan, there is a base for submarines, destroyers, and smaller craft. At Petropavlovsk, on the Kamchatka Peninsula, there is a huge submarine base and several naval air stations. Twenty-five to thirty of Russia's missile-launching submarines, approximately half of the entire Soviet submarine-based nuclear deterrent, operate out of Petropavlovsk. Finally, at Korsakov, near the southern tip of Sakhalin, there is what used to be a minor naval base with a small airfield.

The strategic significance of the region was alluded to on French television by General Gallois, a French strategic specialist. As quoted by Tass, Gallois noted that, "The Soviet armed forces have two zones which may be considered as being top secret; the area of Murmansk in the Kola Peninsula and the zone of the Sea of Okhotsk, where the Kamchatka Peninsula and the island of Sakhalin are situated."[76] Gallois further noted that "a considerable part of the Soviet Navy and intercontinental ballistic missile testing facilities" are located there.

Michael Klare, referring to Russia's Pacific-based submarines, gave further particulars about the strategic significance of the Sea of Okhotsk region: "Many experts believe these vessels are regularly deployed to the relatively protected waters of the Sea of Okhotsk. This and Petropavlovsk would be major targets in nuclear war"[77]— especially, one might add, if one were to attempt a "disarming" first strike against the Soviet Union.

Petropavlovsk, one of these major targets, is vulnerable to air attack by American bombers based on aircraft carriers and, only 500 miles away, in the Aleutians. Another major point of vulnerability is La Perouse Strait, the channel between the Japanese island of Hokkaido and the southern tip of Sakhalin; for it is through this strait, identified by the U.S. Navy as a chokepoint, that the Soviets must pass their mainland-based ships and submarines if they are to be deployed for military operations in the event of impending war.

From the Soviet perspective, it is obviously an objective of the highest urgency to be able to protect their submarines in the Sea of Okhotsk region—and, more particularly, to be able to defend both Petropavlovsk and La Perouse Strait against attack. Accordingly, as we have noted, there are several air bases at Petropavlovsk, together with ground-to-air missiles and other anti-aircraft weaponry. And on Sakhalin, an entire

Soviet army division equipped with antiaircraft guns and missiles stands guard. In recent months, with the nuclear threat from the United States evidently growing, the naval base at Korsakov, guarding La Perouse Strait, has also undergone an expansion described by American and British naval officers as being more rapid than anywhere else in the region.[78]

From the Pentagon's perspective, the strategic problem is precisely the reverse of the problem confronting the Soviet Union: to carry out an unanswerable first strike against the Soviet Union, thus to be able to "fight and win" a nuclear war, the United States must be able to destroy the bulk of Russia's missile-carrying submarines before they can be deployed. This would mean attacking submarines in their bases—Murmansk, Sovetskaya Gavan, and Petropavlovsk. It would mean blocking the La Perouse "chokepoint" and destroying submarines before they can get through it into the Sea of Okhotsk region or the North Pacific. And it would mean attacking missile-launching submarines operating in the relatively protected waters of the Sea of Okhotsk.

It is in this strategic context that the Reagan Administration has been carrying out a major build-up of U.S. forces in the region adjacent to the Sea of Okhotsk. In 1982, Secretary of Defense Caspar Weinberger announced that several squadrons of F-16 fighter planes would be deployed to the huge Misawa airbase in northern Japan—in close striking range of La Perouse Strait and southern Sakhalin. U.S. air forces operating from South Korean bases have also been upgraded with the deployment of late-model fighters. So, too, have U.S. reconnaissance capabilities been strengthened, with U-2, SR-71, EP-3E and E-3A (Awacs) spy planes operating over the Seas of Japan and Okhotsk from bases in Japan, South Korea and Okinawa—also, as we have seen, with RC-135s patrolling continuously off the Kamchatka coast.[79]

Meanwhile, in 1982, the U.S. Navy conducted the first of two large exercises off the Kamchatka coast, designated Norpac Flexops. The exercise, by two U.S. carrier groups doubtless armed with nuclear weapons, received little attention from the Western press. But, as Michael Klare wrote, it "produced so much concern in Moscow that Backfire bombers were sent out to shadow the U.S. fleet and an intelligence satellite was moved into position overhead."[80]

Not long afterwards, in February 1983, *Aviation Week and Space Technology* reported the deployment of U.S. ground-launched cruise missiles to various locations in the region—"to bottle up Soviet forces in the Sea of Japan for destruction by U.S. aircraft."[81] Then, in April, the U.S. Navy conducted maneuvers off the Kamchatka coast—"Operation Fleet Ex '83"—even larger than those carried out the previous year. The exercise involved no fewer than three U.S. carrier groups, with 300 combat aircraft and 23,000 sailors and assault troops. According to Admiral Robert Long, the exercise "was the largest fleet exercise conducted by the Pacific Fleet since World War II."[82]

To be seen in all this were not only preparations for carrying out the Pentagon's first-strike
strategy, should the perceived "necessity" ever
arise: the U.S. build-up in the Sea of Okhotsk
region, and the expansion of provocative military
activities there, are obvious manifestations of a
"get tough" strategy adopted by the Reagan Administration in the spring of 1982. As reported in
mid-April of that year, the Administration at that
time submitted plans to the Senate and House
Armed Service committees, in connection with its
proposed five-year, $1.6 trillion military budget,
calling for a "radically reoriented" U.S. military
strategy. There would be a shift in emphasis away
from a "defensive" to "a more offensively
oriented approach, centered on a greatly ex-
panded Navy that would be able to intervene
anywhere in the world to wage long, multiple
wars against forces of 'the Soviet military empire.'" Such intervention would take place "in
areas of Soviet vulnerability far from the site of
any Soviet aggression"—even in Eastern Europe
and, we can reasonably assume, the Sea of
Okhotsk region. Moreover, "U.S. forces would be
primed for action even if the signs of impending
Soviet aggression were 'ambiguous.'"[83]

Then, on May 21, United Press International's
White House correspondent, Helen Thomas, reported the following:

> A senior White House official said Reagan ap-
> proved an eight-page national security document
> that "undertakes a campaign aimed at internal re-
> form in the Soviet Union and shrinkage of the
> Soviet empire." He affirmed that it could be called
> "a full-court press" against the Soviet Union.[84]

A "full-court press," as basketball fans know, refers to aggressive attempts by players of one team to seize the ball from their opponents in the latter's own end of the court.

In the furor following the shooting down of KAL Flight 007, almost none of this had been visible to the general public. Yet, in the Sea of Okhotsk region, the Reagan Administration had been carrying out an increasingly threatening series of military preparations and maneuvers and had been intensifying its preparations for that day when a "decapitating" first strike against the Soviet Union might become "necessary."

To carry out such a strike, however, the Pentagon must learn everything it can about the air defenses which protect Russia's submarine-based deterrent force in the Sea of Okhotsk region against attack—both to suppress or circumvent those air defense systems, and to disrupt them electronically. For this purpose, those systems must be activated. It was in this context that KAL Flight 007 "carelessly" strayed several hundred miles off course, flew past the air defense systems guarding the huge Soviet submarine base at Petropavlovsk, and then, also by "sheer happenstance," flew across the Sea of Okhotsk straight for the recently strengthened positions guarding La Perouse Strait—where it was finally shot down.

8. THE INTELLIGENCE ROLE OF CIVILIAN AIRLINERS

Some additional background helps to place the KAL airliner incident in clearer perspective. For some years, as we have seen, the task of activating Soviet air defense systems and gathering electronic intelligence about their functioning had been performed by U.S. military aircraft such as the EC-130 shot down over Soviet Armenia—with electronic intelligence stations and/or other aircraft monitoring their flights. As an "intelligence expert" told the *New York Times*, the United States "deliberately planned" flights in the Sea of Okhotsk region "to elicit a Soviet response from the 1950's until reconnaissance tasks were taken over by satellites." Thus, as we have also seen, quite a few such aircraft intruded into Soviet strategic airspace and some were shot down. The same "intelligence expert" added: "We know the Soviets had orders to shoot down our aircraft, and they were always approved in Moscow." He had personal knowledge, he said, that six colonels of Russia's Far East Defense forces were shot "for failure to shoot down our aircraft."[85] The stakes are obviously very high.

But reconnaissance satellites have not, in fact, taken over the entire task of gathering intelligence. They are but one component in an array of facilities, including both ground stations and aircraft such as the RC-135, high-flying U-2 and SR-71 spy planes, and the E-3A (Awacs)—all of which operate in the Sea of Okhotsk region. More particularly, satellites don't activate air defense systems and can't therefore, produce a picture of how they work. This requires an aircraft which actually penetrates Soviet strategic airspace, activating the air defense systems there, while electronic intelligence equipment monitors everything that happens.

But with all these military aircraft available, what possible intelligence role could there be for civilian airliners? A substantial one, it seems. Writing in 1976, John Marks quoted the remarks of Orvis Nelson, "an aviation veteran who worked with the CIA to set up Iran Air in the early 1950s. . . ." Said Nelson: "If I were sitting in a position where I was curious about what was going on in troubled areas, there are two things I would damned well be interested in. The first is information. The second is transportation to get in and out, to get any information and, perhaps, to do some other air activities."[86]

Additional information on the subject began to surface in the Western press in the days after KAL Flight 007 was shot down. The *Miami Herald*, on September 11, reported the observations of various "experts in the field" concerning intelligence advantages to be gained by slow, low overflights:

"In a word: clarity," said one source. He explained, and others confirmed, that satellites able to focus on a fixed spot on earth must be located 23,000 miles above the equator to maintain a stationary orbit. From that distance, clarity is not sufficient to observe details of military hardware.

Low-flying satellites, meanwhile, can observe sites only when they happen to be flying over one of those sites. Their tracks are perfectly predictable, enabling those on the ground to hide the object of attention.

U.S. surveillance aircraft such as the spy plane SR71, flying at 80,000 feet or more, are vulnerable to surface-to-air missiles, as are lower-flying RC135 reconnaissance aircraft if they intrude in unfriendly airspace. Moreover, to attain signals or photos as good as an aircraft at 30,000 feet, the SR71 would require sensors or lenses nearly nine times as strong as those it now possesses . . .

As it happens, quite a few countries have reportedly used civilian airliners for intelligence purposes. Among those identified by various specialists have been Israel's El Al airline, said to have obtained "exquisite information" using commercial flights, and the national airlines of the Soviet Union, Czechoslovakia, Cuba, Libya, and Finland. The attractions of using commercial airliners for intelligence purposes are evident: their normal routes and flying altitudes often take them close enough to military installations so that, with high-resolution cameras and sensors, they can gather intelligence information; the fact that they are commercial airliners provides the intelligence operation with good "cover" and, of considerable importance, provides some protection against attack by the target country's air defense forces.

Ernest Volkman, the national security editor for *Defense Science Magazine*, wrote of this practice: "Everyone in the international airline business winks at it, because they don't want East-West Cold War politics to disrupt an enterprise that requires international cooperation. That's as true of the Eastern bloc as the Western."[87] Thus, Volkman noted, the Soviets are well aware that Finland's Finnair airline routinely spies over Soviet airspace but, because of their sensitive relationship with neutral Finland, have not reacted harshly.[88] On the American side, U.S. interceptors have several times escorted Soviet and Cuban aircraft away from sensitive locations.

The practice of using commercial airliners for intelligence purposes has been sustainable only to the extent that tolerance by the target country has been matched by the spying aircraft's discretion. For example, Czechoslovakia's airline, CSA, requested permission for a "special flight" over Cape Canaveral to coincide with a space shuttle launch. CSA was denied permission for that flight. But then, two Soviet reconnaissance aircraft flew close enough to the Florida coast to "garble up" pre-launch shuttle radio reception, leaving when directed away by the North American Air Defense Command.[89] There have been similar incidents involving CSA and Cubana airliners which strayed into restricted zones of Connecticut and the Hudson Valley while en route between Cuba and Montreal. To avoid being shot down, it has been essential for "straying" aircraft to establish with absolute certainty their identities as commercial airliners, to not push things too far, and to respond to orders by air defense forces as soon as their presence is challenged. By being cautious in these respects, such Socialist-bloc airlines as Aerflot, CSA, and Cubana have managed to avoid serious trouble. But not all airlines have been so lucky. An Israeli airliner with 67 people aboard was shot down over Bulgaria in 1955. And in 1973, the Israelis shot down a Libyan airliner over the Sinai, killing 108 persons aboard.

Not surprisingly, the United States has also used commercial airliners for intelligence purposes. An American official "with close ties to military intelligence" told the *San Francisco Examiner and Chronicle* that "carriers owned by governments deemed friendly to the United States are fitted in this country with cameras and other devices for intelligence collection. The presumption, he said, is that the information will then be shared with the U.S. government."[90]

Quite plainly, one of these airlines is KAL. The airline "is in business," an "authoritative source" told the *Miami Herald*, "because the government wants it to be."[91] Donald Ranard, former director of Korean affairs in the U.S. State Department, further noted that Cho Choong Kun and Cho Chung Hoon, the two brothers who own KAL, have "always had an unholy relationship with the Korean government."[92] KAL also has close ties with the South Korean Air Force, for which it assembles military aircraft and from which it draws almost all of its pilots. And it has close ties as well with the Korean Central Intelligence

Agency (KCIA). Writing in the *Boston Globe*, Fred Kaplan quoted a former CIA official stationed in South Korea for five years as saying: "Anything that the Korean government wanted done that involved international movement involved KAL." The airline moved spies and money in and out of Korea, he said, and senior KCIA officials had also used KAL for personal drug-smuggling operations.[93]

It should not be surprising if KAL, through the KCIA as well as the South Korean Air Force, were also discovered to have connections with U.S. intelligence. The KCIA and the CIA, as a "U.S. military intelligence specialist" told the *Miami Herald*, are "deep in one another's pockets. We established it, designed, provisioned and trained it."[94] There are grounds for suspecting that the CIA had in fact created KAL as well. Orvis Nelson, the aviation veteran who had worked with the CIA to establish Iran Air, told John Marks that he had "set up 16 airlines in his time . . ."[95] *Sixteen* airlines! Although Nelson gave no further details, it is reasonable to assume that he had done most or all of this on contract for the CIA, and that the highest priority had been to create client-country airlines which would operate in strategically important regions—such as those adjacent to the Sea of Okhotsk and Eastern Siberia. Is it not likely that the U.S. Government, which had created both the South Korean Air Force and the KCIA, had also created the airline which was to be found working so closely with those two institutions? It could well be that the

U.S. military intelligence specialist's description
of the CIA-KCIA relationship applies equally to
that between the CIA and KAL—that, "We established it, designed, provisioned and trained it."

Bits and pieces suggesting KAL collaboration
with U.S. intelligence have in fact appeared in the
Western press. On the Canadian Broadcasting
Company, Ernest Volkman stated that KAL
planes regularly overfly Soviet airspace for intelligence purposes. A former U.S. Army intelligence officer also told Fred Kaplan that he "very
clearly" remembered being told by an Air Force
intelligence instructor that KAL was among the
airlines whose planes were sometimes fitted with
"side-view" cameras for intelligence purposes.[96]
A "defense source" told the *San Francisco Examiner and Chronicle* that such cameras, and sen-
soring devices, are installed on various foreign
government-owned airliners at U.S. bases—one
of them being Andrews Air Force Base, near
Washington, D.C. Unidentified U.S. officials who
spoke to the *Examiner* about the use of foreign
airlines for intelligence purposes said they were
"troubled by this activity because innocent passengers, such as those on the KAL flight, might
be killed." Speaking of such activities soon after
Flight 007 was shot down, a Pentagon official told
the *Examiner:* "What's obvious is that no one is
telling us everything they know."[97]

From all this, it seems evident that KAL carried
out missions on behalf of U.S. as well as Korean
intelligence. But would a KAL airliner have
undertaken, for intelligence purposes, a mission
as dangerous as Flight 007's "accidental" over-

flight of Soviet strategic territories proved to be? "There is no evidence," wrote Kaplan, "that South Koreans have ever used 747s loaded with passengers for risky espionage missions."[98] There wouldn't be any very *visible* evidence. But have they not done so? Let us consider the matter further.

9. THE 1978 KAL AIRLINER INCIDENT: AN INSTRUCTIVE PRECEDENT

On April 20, 1978, another KAL airliner, Flight 902, had "accidentally strayed" deep into the other "top secret" region referred to by General Gallois—the area surrounding Murmansk in the Kola Peninsula. That earlier incident was an instructive precedent to the one involving KAL Flight 007, and is worth examining.

In that earlier case, a KAL Boeing 707 bound for Seoul took off from Paris on a polar course which would have led it to Anchorage, Alaska for a refueling stop before proceeding to Seoul. This plane, too, was in the hands of a highly experienced Korean pilot, who had regularly flown the polar route for more than five years.[99] After taking off from Paris at 1:30 p.m. Paris time, the KAL airliner flew on a northwesterly course over the North Sea, with England and Scotland to its left, then flew to the northeast of Iceland and crossed the Greenland coast at Scoresbysund.[100] The plane was last heard from by an amateur radio operator in Canada—the plane's pilot reporting that he was near the Alert station of Canadian Defense Forces on Ellesmere Island, Northwest Territories.[101]

The airliner then passed out of range of any ground control, or tracking, by radar. And it was at this point, about five hours after Flight 902 had left Paris, *that the plane, which had been heading in a northwesterly direction, turned and headed almost in the opposite direction—on a southeasterly course for the Soviet Union.* It flew over the Arctic Ocean and across the Barents Sea north of Russia, entering Soviet airspace from the north. "A rough guess" by the *New York Times* was that "the plane crossed the Soviet coast three hours after the turn after flying southeast 1,500 miles."[102]

The *Times* also noted the strategic importance of the region into which this earlier KAL airliner, like Flight 007, had ostensibly "strayed" through sheer happenstance:

> The Russians are extremely sensitive about foreigners peering into the Murmansk area, which includes the naval base of Severomorsk, headquarters of the Soviet Union's Northern Fleet. Eight air bases in the area are reported to have 60 to 80 long-range and medium-range bombers, and a Western military source said the whole region was "stuffed" with nuclear-warhead missiles.
>
> Nearby is a key base for Soviet nuclear submarines. Two mobile army divisions, plus a brigade of amphibious troops, are along the border and five divisions are reportedly deployed in the Kola Peninsula.[103]

Now let us consider what happened when KAL Flight 902 flew into this region. Years later, after Flight 007 had been shot down, a detailed description of the routine procedures followed by Soviet interceptor pilots in response to intruding aircraft was provided by Dimitri K. Simes. That description, enlarging upon information which appeared in connection with the KAL airliner incidents of both 1978 and 1983, gives us a clearer picture of what evidently happened in both cases; it is worth recounting. Simes, a Russian citizen who later emigrated from the Soviet Union and became a senior fellow at the Carnegie Endowment for International Peace, had lectured to Soviet pilots at Kamchatka in 1969, and they told him how they operate. The appearance of an intruding aircraft, they said, sets in motion a standard procedure. Interceptors are launched and military district headquarters contacted. "No special order is needed, or expected, to force the plane to land. The assumption is that the plane . . . must be forced to land." Interceptor aircraft are instructed, Simes recounted, to identify themselves and make visual contact. If the intruding plane refuses to cooperate, the Soviet pilots "fly in front of it, to be absolutely certain the pilot is aware of what's going on." Then come "warning shots" which, if ignored, are followed by "warning fire . . . to put the onus of decision on the [intruder's] crew." If the pilot has nothing to hide, Simes continued, it is assumed that he will land. Otherwise, the aircraft will be shot down.[104]

The same instructions doubtless apply to Soviet interceptor pilots everywhere; and when unidentified intruding aircraft appear, we have every reason to suppose that those procedures would in fact be followed. What we know about the behavior of the Soviet pilots who intercepted both the 1978 and 1983 KAL airliners suggests that they acted, in both instances, "by the book."

Having noted this, let us return to what happened in 1978, when Flight 007's predecessor, Flight 902, crossed into the "top secret" Murmansk region. Before reaching the Russian mainland, the KAL airliner passed over Franz Josef Land, a group of islands north of Murmansk, and there it was detected by Soviet radar. Russians ground stations attempted repeatedly, by Soviet account, to contact the intruding aircraft, presumably on an international emergency frequency; but they got no answer.[105] The pilot, Kim Chang Kyu, subsequently claimed that his crew didn't hear anything—even as KAL Flight 007, five years later, ostensibly wouldn't "hear anything" as it overflew Kamchatka. Yet we have every reason to suppose that the Soviets, in the circumstances, would do what they said they did.

Then, as the airliner flew over Murmansk, Soviet SU 15 jet fighters scrambled to intercept it. According to the Russian news agency, Tass, the intercepting fighter planes buzzed the airliner "and flooding lights in the darkness, ordered the pilot to follow them to a near-by airfield."[106] How the pilot responded, and what the United States knew about his response, were made clear from a question raised in a *New York Times* account: "Why did the pilot evidently defy the orders of Soviet interceptors and instead take what a State Department spokesman described as evasive action?"[107]

Not only did the KAL pilot take evasive action.

He continued to fly his airliner deeper into Soviet strategic territory, despite the obvious danger to his passengers. The Soviet interceptors flew alongside the airliner as it headed south, trying to get it to land. But the intruding aircraft, by the Soviet account, ignored their signals to do so. This was also confirmed by former C.I.A. Director Stansfield Turner: "When the Soviets gave the signals, the pilot didn't obey."[108]

The Korean crew claimed afterwards that they hadn't understood the Soviet signals. In fact, international aviation rules call for an interceptor to warn an intruding aircraft at night by flashing its lights at irregular intervals while dipping its wings; the intruding aircraft is obliged to respond by flashing its own navigational and landing lights, and to follow the interceptor—either to an airfield or away from prohibited airspace. All aircraft, including Soviet and South Korean, operate by these same rules. Thus, the explanation given by Flight 902's pilot would have been like a motorist, seeing a highway patrolman's flashing red light in his rear view mirror, stepping on the gas in an effort to get away and protesting after he was caught that he didn't know what the flashing red light meant.

Kim, in any case, continued to ignore the signals coming from the interceptors. "Then," as Kevin Close wrote in the *Washington Post*, "a fighter fired a burst of shells across the airliner's nose as a warning to land. When it continued flying south, Soviet ground controllers ordered the liner fired on."[109] The entire sequence of actions on the Soviet side, as we can see, followed precisely the description of Soviet procedures given some years earlier to Dimitri Simes by Russian pilots based on Kamchatka.

By the most conservative calculations, Kim had flown for 18 minutes into Soviet airspace—approximately 150 miles at 500 miles per hour—by the time the order to fire upon his plane was carried out. A Soviet interceptor, firing a cannon round, struck the passenger compartment. The exploding shell killed two passengers and decompressed the compartment, whereupon Kim took the plane into an emergency dive. Descending from 35,000 to 3,000 feet, he continued his flight into Soviet airspace, ostensibly "searching for a suitable place to land." Finally, he brought the plane to an emergency landing near Kem, south of Murmansk—by which time he had flown some 300 miles into this "top secret" Soviet strategic region.

We have, in addition to the question of why Kim evidently defied Soviet orders to land, the question of how this earlier KAL airliner could also have "strayed" so far from its course to end up where it did. According to the *New York Times,*"The South Korean Embassy in Helsinki was reported to have blamed navigation errors, but a Korean Air Lines navigator in Seoul said that was unthinkable because the plane was too far off course."[110] The President of Korean Air Lines, Cho Choon-Hoon, noted that the pilot had previously flown over the North Pole 70 times without incident. The airliner's crew told him, he said, that the plane had gone off course after "an electrical shock paralyzed the navigation system."[111] In the version given by the navigator after his release, both the gyrocompass and Loran had failed.

Had the navigation system been paralyzed by an electrical shock, the crew doubtless would have perceived it to be inoperative. Yet the pilot and co-pilot said they had been misled by erroneous readings which that system, for unexplained reasons, ostensibly began to give out just before the plane turned away from the course it had been on. The co-pilot was quoted as saying that "the crew somehow became disoriented while flying north of the Karelia Peninsula. Their instruments seemed to be indicating they were in a safe flight path outside Soviet air space, but they began seeing an unfamiliar land mass beneath them." And the pilot, Kim, told the passengers after the emergency landing that "he had made a terrible mistake, ignoring a '6th sense' that told him his course was in error even though the navigation equipment said it was right." He also said he had "steered south" after the plane's emergency descent to 3,000 feet, searching for a suitable landing area.[112] He didn't explain how he had "steered south," which he had indeed, with navigation equipment which had previously taken him in a direction almost the opposite of where he thought he had been headed.

Elsewhere, the "failed navigation equipment" explanation had been discounted from the outset. In Anchorage, Alaska, Frances Walker of KAL had expressed astonishment upon learning where the airliner had gone down: "I don't understand it, not with the navigation equipment he has got." And in Washington, "authorities" said that a breakdown in navigational equipment was unlikely "because of the sophistication and duplication of the equipment"—which in this case, as with the Boeing 747 shot down more recently over Sakhalin, included back-up systems to cross-check the primary navigation system.[113]

And there was one circumstance which could not be explained away with stories of "electrical shocks" and grossly erroneous readings which the navigation equipment suddenly began to give out. When the plane was flying beyond Greenland, just before its turn, it had been late afternoon and the weather had been clear with only a few scattered clouds. As one can see on the map showing the course taken by Flight 902, the sun was ahead and to the left of the aircraft before its turn and was behind and to the right afterwards. Days later, when passengers from the downed airliner finally arrived at their destinations, *Washington Post* correspondent William Chapman filed this report about passenger reactions when the plane turned: "Several of the passengers said yesterday in Tokyo that they had become concerned when they noticed that the plane, which had been flying toward the setting sun, was suddenly flying away from it."[114]

It is inconceivable that the highly experienced crew had not noticed the same thing. Nor is it conceivable that they hadn't known that Flight 902's estimated time of arrival in Anchorage, after passing over the polar region into a zone of growing light, was about noon, Anchorage time. And yet, after turning away from the sun, Flight

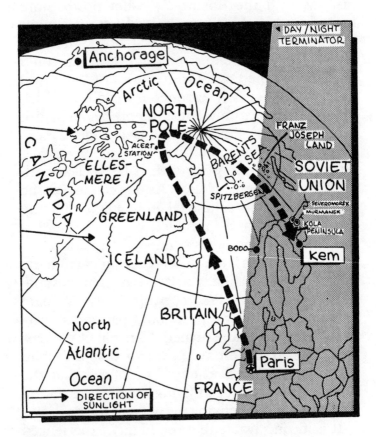

Map: Paul Gordon
Sources: *New York Times;* Steven Soter

902's pilot flew for three hours towards the darkness encroaching from the east before entering into Soviet airspace.[115] Furthermore, the pilot did this without informing anyone that he was "lost" or had experienced a "navigation equipment failure."

We can only conclude that the "failed navigation equipment" stories had been hogwash. The pilot had to know the general direction he was headed in, and he manifestly stayed on that southeasterly course because it was his intention to do so. The case here was very clear-cut. There could not possibly have been a "finger error" in programming the INS, or inadvertent flight on a "constant magnetic heading," or navigational "carelessness" while skirting Soviet territories along a normal airline route, or decision to "take a short-cut to Seoul."

The object of Kim Chang Kyu's intent could be readily deduced from where his course took him to, out of all the directions in which an "off course" plane might have gone. As the *Washington Post* reported, the KAL airliner "was shot down after passing over Murmansk at 35,000 feet. Murmansk is the base for the Soviet Union's intercontinental ballistic missile submarine fleet and center for other major military operations."[116] Quite evidently, the KAL pilot had flown his "civilian airliner" on a mission for the intelligence services of the only power which might plausibly have instigated such a mission— the United States. There could be no other remotely plausible explanation for why the pilot would have embarked upon such a drastic and

lengthy digression from his normal course, flying
where he did, and persisting in his deep penetration into Soviet strategic airspace despite the risk
to his plane and passengers.

And in fact, American intelligence reaped
great benefits from the KAL airliner's flight over
Soviet territory. A "high American intelligence
source" told CBS Evening News, as Dan Rather
reported after KAL Flight 007 was shot down in
1983, that this earlier KAL flight "went so deep
into Soviet strategic territory it pointed out to the
West the serious weaknesses in the Soviet air defense system—so much so that key Soviet defense
officials were fired, some even executed." Plainly,
this had not come to American intelligence as
"manna from heaven."

Nor were American officials as circumspect in
1978, as they would be in 1983, about telling
what they knew and how they came to know it.
On April 20, 1978, the day the KAL airliner went
down, Administration and Pentagon officials
"who asked not to be identified, said that based
on radar tracking they 'have reason to believe'
the plane had entered Soviet airspace and was on
the ground in a remote corner of the Soviet
Union."[117] The next day, it will be recalled, a State
Department spokesman had also spoken of the
evasive action taken by the airliner when, upon
entering Soviet airspace, it was met by Soviet interceptors. Both of these statements showed that
the United States had been closely following the
Korean airliner's flight into this "top secret"
Soviet strategic region as it occurred—even as

U.S. intelligence had monitored the EC-130 flight into Soviet Armenia some years earlier.

Norwegian military sources at the Bodo, Norway listening post also told United Press International "that they tracked the plane approximately 200 miles inside Soviet territory when it disappeared from their radar screen"—apparently when it was hit by the gunfire which decompressed the passenger compartment and caused the pilot to dive from 35,000 to 3,000 feet. By the Norwegian account, the plane had been in Soviet airspace for about an hour by the time this happened.[118] So in this earlier incident, too, Western intelligence facilities tracked the errant KAL airliner on its flight into Soviet strategic airspace and did nothing, by anyone's account, to warn the pilot away from his dangerous course.

There was an even more telling revelation. On April 21, when the Soviets had yet to say anything about how the airliner had been forced down, President Jimmy Carter's National Security Adviser, Zbigniew Brzezinski, told reporters that Soviet jet interceptors "had apparently fired at the South Korean airliner," forcing it to land in western Russia.[119] Five days later the *New York Times* reported that Brzezinski's remark had "upset and troubled intelligence specialists who say that Mr. Brzezinski may have breached security."

When asked about this, a National Security Council spokesman told the *Times* that Brzezinski had been citing a published report by Jiji Press, the Japanese News agency. But Brzezinski had said nothing of the Jiji Press in his remarks to reporters. And if that news agency had carried any such report, it would have had to have been after Brzezinski's "security breach." For the attack on the airliner had not been revealed until the next day, when the repatriated passengers told the story upon reaching Helsinki.

The "intelligence officials" interviewed by the *New York Times* quite evidently knew what the United States was doing during the Korean airliner's intrusion—and also knew where Mr. Brzezinski, who oversaw covert operations for President Carter in his capacity of National Security Adviser, had obtained his information. Those officials said that, "Mr. Brzezinski apparently obtained his information about the Soviet attack . . . through secret monitoring of Soviet conversations and a reading of radio conversations between Soviet pilots."[120]

Again, what we have seen here was clearly an American-inspired flight by the KAL airliner over Murmansk and deep into the surrounding strategic region. U.S. intelligence had followed that flight closely from the outset, had known precisely what was going on, and quite obviously had done nothing to discourage the pilot from continuing on his dangerous course. As a result, American intelligence officials learned a great deal—not only about the weaknesses of the air defense system guarding Murmansk and the region beyond it, but also about the operation of that system.

Moreover, U.S. intelligence had discovered a "solution" for the problem created by Soviet interceptors and ground-to-air missiles—how to achieve the deep penetration of a "top secret" Soviet strategic region, activating the air defenses which guard it, without getting the intruding aircraft immediately shot down. That "solution" had taken the form of a civilian airliner flying at night, whose ambiguous identity allowed it to get much farther, under the pretense of having "strayed," than would ever have been possible for a military reconnaissance plane. KAL Flight 902 had "gotten away" with a major intelligence coup.

It is taken for granted, of course, that intelligence operations are often a risky business. But in this case there had been much less of an international furor than there would be in 1983, when KAL Flight 007 was shot down. "Only" two passengers had been killed as a result of the 1978 overflight, a Japanese and a Korean. Their deaths had caused no visible grief in the United States and had been overshadowed in the media by stories of the return to safety of the remaining passengers. Indeed, the strongest American complaint took place when, in Murmansk, American and Japanese officials had engaged the Soviets in a "heated confrontation" bitterly protesting the temporary detention of the airliner's pilot and navigator for questioning.[121]

For their part the Soviets, as we have noted, "are extremely sensitive about foreigners peering into the Murmansk area." But they had also been "eager to avoid a major uproar over the Korean plane's incursion, in part because of the presence in Moscow of Cyrus R. Vance, the American Secretary of State, who is discussing disarmament with Soviet leaders."[122] Accordingly, the passengers had been quickly taken to Murmansk, where a Pan American airliner had flown them on to their destinations in Japan and Korea. After questioning the pilot and navigator for several days, the Soviets had also "pardoned" them for their illegal intrusion into Soviet airspace and they had been released as well. To top things off, Korean President Park Chung Hee had expressed his "deep gratitude" to the Soviets for the speedy return of the surviving passengers.[123] Thus, in the larger strategic game being played, the benefits derived from the KAL airliner's flight into Soviet strategic airspace had been very substantial indeed—and the costs presumably would have been considered minimal.

But there had always been the possibility that the KAL airliner would be shot down and its passengers killed. In that case there surely would have been an uproar over the affair, as there would be when KAL Flight 007 was shot down in 1983. The 1978 flight had taken place precisely at the moment when Secretary of State Cyrus Vance was in Moscow for disarmament talks with the Soviet leaders. A major incident would certainly have wrecked the prospects for any progress in those talks—even as the ill-fated flight of an American U-2 reconnaissance plane over Russia in May 1960, two weeks before the Berlin summit conference, had wrecked that summit conference. It seems highly unlikely that Vance himself would have approved of the KAL overflight at that time, probably at any time. But had

Zbigniew Brzezinski, the President's overseer of covert operations? If not, who had? These are among the unanswered questions raised by the 1978 KAL airliner incident, and the answers would surely have important implications for the manner in which U.S. foreign policy is conducted.

In any case, the "successful operation" in 1978, and the lessons U.S. intelligence learned from it, form an important part of the background for what happened five years later.

10. KAL FLIGHT 007: AN EXPLANATION

The Nation, editorializing about KAL Flight 007's "accidental straying" into Soviet airspace, observed that, "The odds against the airliner's computerized navigational system malfunctioning with such exquisite symmetry as to steer it over the sensitive Russian military and telecommunications installations in the northwest Pacific are astronomical."[124] What, then, is to be said about the odds against *two* aircraft operated by the same airlines each "accidentally straying" precisely over vital Soviet naval installations on opposite sides of the globe—the one being obliged to fly almost in the opposite direction from where it was headed in order to accomplish its feat?

We can't expect the U.S. National Security Agency to present us with a smoking gun; quite obviously, those responsible for operations of this sort do everything possible to cover their tracks. But when we add the circumstances surrounding the 1978 KAL airliner incident to those surrounding Flight 007's penetration of Soviet strategic airspace in 1983, it seems to me that we can come to only one conclusion—that both flights had been instigated by U.S. intelligence for the evident purpose, perhaps among others, of studying the operation of the air defenses guarding vital Soviet naval installations. Moreover, this would have been in the context of the Pentagon's strenuous effort to develop its capabilities for destroying Russia's missile-launching submarine fleet before it can be brought into operation, thus to be able to carry out an unanswerable nuclear attack against the Soviet Union.

Logically, what happened in September 1983 was essentially this. U.S. intelligence had re-cruited Chun Byung In and Sohn Dong Hui, both former South Korean Air Force pilots, for the mission. Chun Byung In was not the careless, incompetent pilot the ICAO scenarios required him to be. He was, in fact, a meticulous, highly skilled aviator, and it was precisely for this reason that he would have been chosen for the mission. As with Francis Gary Powers, pilot of the ill-fated U-2 flight over Russia in May 1960, the induce-ments had probably been very good money and the sense of doing something of great impor-tance—in this case, on behalf of South Korea's American patrons. Without that patronage a man like Chun Byung In, a pilot in the U.S.-created South Korean Air Force before he be-came a highly esteemed KAL pilot, would almost certainly never have gotten to where he did in life. Once drawn into cooperation with his American benefactors, he would probably have found it difficult, whatever his better judgement might have told him, to say "No" to a "highly important mission."

It is also very possible, though not certain, that
Flight 007's mission had been sanctioned by
higher KAL authority. U.S. intelligence doubtless
enjoyed a working relationship with "Charlie
Cho" and "Harry Cho," the two brothers who
own KAL; the practice of using KAL airliners for
various South Korean and American intelligence
purposes must have had their acquiescence. And
recall Kim Chang Kyu's highly risky penetration
of Soviet airspace in 1978, ending in a crash landing and the deaths of two passengers. Kim remained a pilot in good standing at KAL, suggesting that he hadn't "done anything wrong" where
its owners were concerned. The fact that Kim
Chang Kyu and Chun Byung In would both
undertake dangerous and "strictly forbidden"
flights into Soviet strategic airspace suggests
something about what they understood the position of KAL's management to be.

We have already seen how implausible it was
that Flight 007 might have deviated from its assigned course upon leaving Anchorage, through
a programming error, and then, through a whole
series of navigational errors, flew unwittingly all
the way to the point off southern Sakhalin where
it was shot down. But the Korean airliner, as the
ICAO had said, indeed began its deviation from
its assigned course shortly after leaving Anchorage. David Pearson's account in *The Nation* provides us with specific details:

> About ten miles west of Anchorage, KAL 007
> began to diverge from a direct course to Bethel,
> Alaska, and was six miles to the north of its nor-
> mal route at the limit of civilian air-traffic control.

The Anchorage controllers said they did not consider this important because they assumed the airliner would correct its course when it picked up
the VOR radio beacon at Bethel, several hundred
miles to the west.

When the airliner passed Bethel, its pilot reported to air traffic control that he had flown
over Bethel on course. In fact, the Air Force
radar station at King Salmon showed that Flight
007 was already some twelve nautical miles north
of where its pilot said he was. Chun, having
falsely reported his position to Anchorage, was
already beginning to conceal where he was going.

Pearson notes that under an agreement between the Federal Aviation Administration and
the Defense Department, Alaska-based military
radar stations are required to verify that airliners
are on course as they fly westward from Alaska.
"If they deviate, military radar operators are to
notify the FAA, which in turn radios the airliner."
The King Salmon data about Flight 007, according to the ICAO final report, was sent to Anchorage air traffic control. This data made it clear
that the airliner was continuing to fly off-course,
calling for an immediate reaction by Anchorage
air traffic control. But for unexplained reasons,
the data "was not presented to controllers."

By the time Flight 007 had approached the
limits of military radar coverage at Cape
Newenham, Alaska, it was at least sixty-five miles
off course—at least twenty-five times the maxi-
mum permissible error of two nautical miles per
hour for its INS. This deviation, showing that the
airliner was headed for Kamchatka, doubtless

appeared on Cape Newenham's radar; and it was that station's duty to inform the FAA of any such deviation. But the Cape Newenham station remained silent.[125]

Some time afterwards, when Flight 007 was nearing its rendezvous with the RC-135 off the northeast coast of Kamchatka, its pilot reported that he was at the Neeva waypoint—though his VOR, tuned into Shemya, would have shown that he was nowhere near where he said he was. And the giant phased-array radar at Shemya would have shown the airliner to be headed straight for the Kamchatka coast. But the Shemya base sounded no alarms either. These several sins of commission and omission, necessary to facilitate the airliner's uninterrupted flight on its unauthorized course, could not *all* have been by accident. Beyond reasonable doubt, they had been by design.

Then began the active phase of the airliner's mission. In overflying Kamchatka and southern Sakhalin, Flight 007 had two evident objectives: to activate the Soviet air defenses guarding Petropavlovsk, where the bulk of Russia's Pacific submarine fleet is based, together with those at Korsakov, guarding La Perouse Strait. Soviet Marshal Nikolai Ogarkov asserted that, following its "rendezvous" with the RC-135 off the Kamchatka coast, "the second plane went straight to Petropavlovsk . . ." Whether Flight 007 flew right over Petropavlovsk or not, it was the air defense systems guarding that base and southern Kamchatka more generally which would have been, and in fact were, activated.

Furthermore, U.S. intelligence doubtless knew exactly what was going on. As we have seen, continuous patrolling by RC-135 reconnaissance planes and the presence of other electronic intelligence facilities give the United States "routine, 24-hour-a-day, 365-day-a-year [sic] intercept coverage of sensitive and important target areas"—such as the Murmansk and Sea of Okhotsk regions. Therefore, we are justified in concluding with Bernard and Eskelson, the former RC-135 intelligence specialists, that:

> Within these capabilities of the RC-135 lie the precise reasons we believe that the entire sweep of events—from the time the Soviets first began tracking KAL Flight 007, to 'confusing' it with the American reconnaissance aircraft, to the moment Soviet fighter planes sitting on Soviet airfields were ordered to go from "standby" to "alert" status due to the potential penetration of their airspace by an "intruder aircraft," to the time of the shootdown—was meticulously monitored and analyzed instantaneously by U.S. intelligence.[126]

And why was Flight 007 not warned off its dangerous course? Not, as U.S. intelligence officials had suggested to the press, because there was no system "merging" the day-to-day work of the intelligence community with that of "the airline control people." As Bernard and Eskelson have told us, the RC-135 is capable of communicating with both civilian aircraft and air traffic controllers. They further noted that RC-135s had transmitted real-time warnings to American aircraft operating over North Vietnam, alerting them when they were being tracked by hostile radar and, in some cases, even helping U.S. pilots to evade ground or air-launched missiles about to be fired at them.[127]

Logically, U.S. intelligence authorities failed to warn Flight 007 for the same, entirely evident reason they had not warned the KAL airliner which overflew Murmansk five years earlier—because both flights had been on missions for the National Security Agency. We can also reasonably conclude that the RC-135, which carries equipment for "jamming" radar and radio transmission, had used these capabilities for "confusing" Soviet air defenses on Kamchatka just as they had done in Vietnam.

The requirements of an intelligence mission would also explain Chun Byung In's own "strange" behavior: his unresponsiveness to attempts by another KAL airliner, and doubtless by the Soviets as well, to make radio contact; the incorrect position which he had given to Japanese air traffic controllers; the fact that, during at least part of his flight, he had apparently flown with his air navigation lighs off; the fact that he had manifestly turned off his IFF, by which his aircraft could have been immediately identified when it intruded into Soviet airspace over Kamchatka. After Flight 007 had been shot down, Kevin Close of the *Washington Post* wrote this about the similarity between Chun Byung In's actions and those of Kim Chang Kyu, five years earlier: "The 1978 incident was duplicated, almost step-by-step, by Flight 007 Wednesday."[128] This, too, could not have been "sheer coincidence." Quite obviously, the two pilots had followed very similar pre-planned tactics to evade attempts by Soviet air defense forces to get them to land.

And Chun clearly knew exactly where he was going. After overflying Kamchatka, he had flown on a line which took him straight toward the recently strengthened Soviet defensive positions at Korsakov—the second objective of his mission. Once past southern Sakhalin, Flight 007 would have continued on its course to Seoul.

But the Soviets had been forewarned by his Kamchatka overflight, made possible by various evasive maneuvers, and when his plane reached southern Sakhalin, Soviet jet fighters were there to intercept him. According to Marshal Ogarkov, "The actions [of the intruding aircraft] in this stage became defiant. No matter what attempts were made to contact it . . . it did not respond to signals from Soviet interceptor planes. Moreover, it began to maneuver, changing its speed and altitude of flight, obviously trying to evade the Soviet airplane."[129] Elaborating on this, the Soviet Defense Ministry newspaper *Krasnaya Zvezda* asserted that Flight 007 had resorted to a maneuver typically employed by U.S. spy planes to evade Soviet air defenses: at a critical moment of the pursuit the airliner had lowered its flaps to decrease speed, trying to make the Soviet fighter overshoot so the airliner could "slip away."[130] The Reagan Administration itself made public transcripts of tape-recorded exchanges between Soviet pilots and ground control which tended to corroborate the essential correctness of these Soviet claims; those exchanges had the Soviet pilot who shot down the airliner reporting at one point that the aircraft was "decreasing speed," causing the jet fighter to move ahead of it.

The Soviet side provided further details when, on September 10, Russian television conducted interviews with three pilots who had been sent up to intercept the intruding aircraft, including the pilot who shot the airliner down. That latter pilot, whose name was not given, "described his certainty that he was dealing with an 'enemy aircraft,' and told how he had wagged his plane's wings and fired four bursts of tracer shells along the jetliner's route." The *New York Times* account of the interview continues:

> "This in international code signifies that 'you're an intruder,'" he said. "He had to answer somehow that 'yes, I'm an intruding aircraft and in trouble,' and I would've helped him if he was in trouble, and if he was an intruder he could have landed on our airfield and we would have sorted it out."
>
> But he kept flying on the same course and at the same altitude, and I received a command, a precise and definite command," the pilot said.[131]

Earlier, on September 3, U.S. officials had given information to the *Washington Post* confirming the accuracy of the Soviet pilot's account. There were "obscure" portions of the taped conversations from which, they said, "a deduction could be made that a Soviet fighter may have circled in front of the Korean Air Lines plane and may have wiggled its wings."[132] These "obscure" passages, which would have shown that Soviet interceptors had followed established international procedures for warning intruding aircraft, did not appear in the transcripts released by the Reagan Administration; recall that the Administration had released those transcripts to demonstrate that the Soviets had inexplicably shot down a civilian airliner in cold blood.

But the State Department, on the day after the Soviet television interviews, released an amended version of the tape transcript which had the Soviet pilot reporting, six minutes before he shot the airliner down, that he had "broken off lock-on" and was "firing cannon bursts."[133] This, too, lent support to Soviet claims that the pilot had fired warning bursts of tracer shells before shooting the intruding aircraft down. The sequence of Soviet actions, from beginning to end, closely followed the operating instructions described many years earlier to Dimitri Simes by Russian pilots then based on Kamchatka. But Chun Byung In, like Kim Chang Kyu before him, ignored even the cannon bursts fired as a final warning. Rudolph Braunberg, the former Lufthansa pilot, noted the implications of Chun's refusal "to comply with the Soviet request—most certainly made—to land on a military airfield in Sakhalin . . ."

> He violated all internal and international regulations. All airline pilots are strictly instructed to follow planes ordering them to land if they have entered another nation's prohibited airspace . . . Every pilot knows that disobeying an interceptor while in prohibited airspace means risking being shot down. Disregarding it or trying to sneak back

into international airspace is seen as a suicidal attempt by every responsible pilot, and is strictly
forbidden by the airlines.[134]

Chun's motive for flying on, at least in part,
could be deduced from the remarks made on
television by the Soviet pilot who shot his plane
down: "I fired four tracer shells right next to
him, but there was no reaction. If we could have
landed him at the airport, we could have discovered everything behind this."[135] Chun was
plainly determined not to let that happen. So,
even after the warning shots had been fired, he
flew on for another six minutes (approximately
50 miles at 500 miles per hour)—at one point
resorting to the evasive maneuvers described
above. Chun's plane managed almost to exit
from Soviet airspace once again. But at this point
the Soviet pilot fired the missile which brought
the airliner down. What we have seen here is a
pilot who had known what he was about and had
been very determined to accomplish an extremely serious purpose—despite the great risks
to his plane and all those aboard. Chun Byung
In, the former South Korean Air Force pilot, had
evidently remained a warrior to the end.

In the same way, the U.S. intelligence officials
who doubtless followed the entire drama had
plainly been truer to their cold war duties, as they
considered them to be, than to any considerations of risk to innocent lives; everyone had followed orders. Thus, there had been no warning
to Flight 007 or anyone else from the Wakkanai
electronic intelligence station, which had most

certainly listened to every word spoken by the Soviet pilots from only a few miles away.

From the intelligence perspective, the Korean airliner's flight paid off handsomely: the American interest in "casing out" the air defense systems guarding the Petropavlovsk submarine base and La Perouse Strait was very well served. As for the risks, the U.S. intelligence officials concerned, like Chun Byung In, had doubtless convinced themselves that the airliner, after overflying southern Sakhalin, would make it safely back into international airspace. But Flight 007's pilot, his crew, and the more than two hundred passengers who had been taken along for the ride did not, in fact, quite make it.

11. WHY THE SOVIETS ACTED AS THEY DID

We are still left with the question of how the Soviets could have shot down a civilian airliner in what seemed to be such a brutal manner. When Flight 007 went down, White House spokesman Larry Speakes spoke of "the disgust that the entire world feels at the utter barbarity of the action of the Soviet Government in shooting down an unarmed, nonmilitary passenger plane . . ." And President Ronald Reagan, protesting "the Soviet attack on an unarmed civilian passenger plane," said that, "Words can scarcely express our revulsion at this horrifying act of violence."[136] Administration spokesmen subsequently asserted that "the Soviet military had had ample time to discern that the plane they had tracked into their airspace was a commercial jetliner" and that "there was no way the Russians could have mistaken the identity of the plane at the time they shot it down."[137] A State Department official added that, "We understand Soviet paranoia and inordinate sensitivity about the inviolability of air space and territorial waters. But planes, civilian and military, do fly off course. When Russian and Cuban planes went off course over the United States in years past, we didn't shoot them down, we led them back on course and suspended their flight privileges for a while."[138] How, then, was it possible that the Soviets could do what they did?

The answer, as it turned out, was that they evidently did not know that the intruding aircraft was a civilian airliner and had every reason to believe, *on the basis of its behavior,* that it was an American intelligence plane. On October 7, five weeks after Flight 007 was shot down, the *New York Times* reported "United States intelligence experts" as saying that "they have reviewed all available evidence and found no indication that Soviet air defense personnel knew that it was a commercial airliner before the attack." These intelligence experts, "using transcripts of Soviet radio transmissions, radar impulses and additional intelligence data that American and Japanese officials refuse to discuss publicly," had concluded that the SU-15 fighter which shot down the airliner had fired its rockets from behind and below it; "given the difficulty of identifying a plane from below, they believed the Soviet pilot probably did not know what kind of plane he was shooting down in Soviet airspace."[139] Had the airliner in any way identified himself to the Soviets, either through its IFF or by responding to Russian attempts to contact it, or had the intercepted Soviet radio transmissions revealed any thoughts that the intruding aircraft was a civilian airliner, these "intelligence officials" doubtless would have said so.

In the absence of any information about the intruding aircraft's identity, either from Western ground controllers or from the plane itself, the

Soviets necessarily reached conclusions about its identity and purposes based on past experience as well as its behavior. That past experience, it will be recalled, included "aggressive" American intelligence operations in the Sea of Okhotsk region, including deliberate flights into Soviet strategic airspace by American reconnaissance aircraft.

In this regard, the September 10 Soviet television broadcast showed footage of "twin-jet Sukhoi interceptors with long green noses and a white rocket under each wing scrambling under falling sleet to intercept what the reporter said was an American reconnaissance plane that had approached Soviet territory and then swerved away at the last moment. There are dozens of such incidents each day, he said, and this is how the Americans 'constantly play on our nerves.' "[140] Whether dozens of times each day or not, we have it from the American side that it is common practice to "tickle" Soviet air defenses in this way. Such was the context in which the unidentified aircraft, evidently after having rendezvoused with the RC-135, had intruded into Soviet airspace.

And this is how Marshal Ogarkov described the process by which the Soviets reached the conclusion they did about the aircraft's identity:

> The whole analysis of the behavior of that aircraft, its route, the nature of its flight and our analysis of the interaction between this plane in the Kamchatka area and its choice of course in the direction of the most significant military installations . . . and, finally, a sort of incomprehensible

conduct consisting in total ignoring of all warning and cautionary signals . . . And let me add that all command levels—we reached the total conviction that we were dealing with a reconnaissance plane and we were trying to force it to land in Kamchatka. But when it did not react to 120 warning shots, nothing was left to us but act the way we did.[141]

Given its behavior during its long flight across this "top secret" Soviet strategic region, and the absence of signs from anywhere identifying the intruding aircraft as a civilian airliner, is it reasonable to suppose that the Soviets would have reached any conclusion other than the one they arrived at? On all the evidence, Flight 007 was *both* a civilian airliner *and* a plane on an intelligence mission. The only aspect of that aircraft presented to the general public by the Reagan Administration, quite naturally, was its identity as a civilian airliner. Hence the understandable expressions of outrage focussed entirely on the Soviet Union. But the only aspect of the aircraft which presented itself to the Soviets was that of a reconnaissance plane flying over their most sensitive strategic positions in the region, and that is what the Soviets believed they were shooting down.

Here we also see the fatal contradiction in what we can reasonably presume was the plan to use KAL Flight 007 for intelligence purposes. Its intelligence cover was that of a civilian airliner and its identification as such—or the uncertainty about its identity—might have been expected to deter the Soviets from shooting it down. But its chances for accomplishing both phases of its long mission required it to make itself as invisible as possible, concealing its identity as a civilian airliner, and to resort to maneuvers which would inevitably lead the Soviets to conclude that it was an intelligence aircraft.

But how about the observation made by American officials that the United States, instead of shooting down off-course Russian and Cuban planes, had "led them back on course and suspended their flight priviledges for a while."? It has been suggested that those Russian and Cuban airliners might also have "accidentally strayed" for intelligence purposes—and indeed they might have. The difference is that those planes, all of them apparently on daytime flights, *allowed themselves to be led back on course*—in the process ensuring their passengers against harm. KAL Flight 007, like the KAL airliner which penetrated the Murmansk region in 1978, did just the opposite: by evading every Soviet effort to get it to turn away or land, it forced upon the Soviets the choice of shooting it down or accepting the principle that unidentified aircraft could penetrate Soviet strategic airspace with impunity simply by ignoring every effort to warn such aircraft away or force them to land.

Even so staunch a cold warrior as retired General George J. Keegan, formerly chief of U.S. Air Force Intelligence, would say of "the Koreans" upon learning that KAL Flight 007 had been shot down: "What happened today they invited."[142] It was Flight 007's pilot, and quite evidently U.S. intelligence as well, who knew that

the aircraft which flew into Soviet strategic airspace was a civilian airliner—and who forced
upon the Soviets the choice of shooting it down
or letting it fly through that airspace with impunity. Can we Americans avoid asking ourselves
whether any action of that kind by our own
officials is morally or legally tolerable? I think
not.

There is one other aspect of the Soviet response which requires comment—the suggestion
that it was an expression of Soviet "paranoia" and
"oversensitivity." Viktor A. Linnik, a consultant
to the Soviet Communist Party's Central Committee, would himself suggest, in the politically
embarrassing aftermath of the airliner incident,
that with U.S. reconnaissance planes "flying over
the area all the time," the Soviet pilots had
reacted in a "trigger-happy manner."[143] There
was implied criticism here of the Soviet military's
handling of the intrusion. And of course it is true
that the Soviet leadership has shown signs of
paranoia; their over-reaction to even modest expressions of domestic dissent provides plenty of
evidence of that. But to ascribe their actions in
the airliner incident to paranoia, an understandable conclusion if one presumes the innocence of
Flight 007's passage into Soviet airspace and is
unaware of the strategic significance of the positions overflown by the airliner, is not only to read
this particular Soviet reaction wrongly; it fails to
understand the full seriousness of the strategic
game being played.

The Soviet military's reaction was not in fact
paranoid. They are fully aware of the aggressive

American intelligence effort to penetrate the Sea of Okhotsk region; and they are also very certainly aware of the Pentagon's efforts to perfect its capabilities for destroying Russia's missile-launching submarine force in the context of the Reagan Administration's proclaimed intent "to build a capacity to fight [and doubtless 'win'] nuclear wars that range from a limited strike through a protracted conflict to an all-out exchange."[144]

It is this context which gives reconnaissance aircraft intruding into both the Murmansk and Sea of Okhotsk regions their strategic significance. And this was certainly how the Soviet military saw the situation, as shown by Marshal Ogarkov's response when asked at his news conference: "Do you think that the protection of the sacred borders of the Soviet Union was worth the lives of 269 persons aboard the jetliner?" Ogarkov replied:

> Protection of the sacred, inviolable borders of our country, and our political system, was worth to us—as you know very well—many, many millions of lives and it was exactly preservation of our borders, of our frontiers and our system and we would not add to the list of those millions the 269 victims of those who victimized those people for reasons other than the defense of the sacred frontiers. Those other people should be asked why.[145]

The threat posed to Soviet security by the Pentagon's attempts to perfect its anti-submarine warfare capabilities is an extremely serious one. Moreover, with tens of thousands of nuclear weapons poised for launching, the struggle for survival must be won by the Soviet Union (not to mention the United States and, indeed, all of humanity) before the button is pressed to start World War III. Once that happens, it will be too late to "defend" any nation that is attacked. However one might choose to judge their actions, these were the circumstances in which the Soviet military command deliberately shot down the unidentified aircraft which intruded into Soviet strategic airspace over Kamchatka and southern Sakhalin—killing the crew and the 246 passengers whom they didn't know were aboard.

12. THE THINKING OF AMERICA'S LEADERS

And what about our own leaders? The circumstances surrounding KAL Flight 007's penetration of Soviet strategic airspace point, beyond any reasonable doubt, to the conclusion that it was on a U.S. intelligence mission; but many Americans will find it difficult to swallow the idea that our own leaders would be capable of taking such a gamble with the lives of innocent airline passengers. We are ready enough to believe that the Soviets would knowingly shoot down a civilian passenger plane in cold blood. In other situations, as in Afghanistan, the Soviets have indeed shown themselves capable of being ruthless. But is it really conceivable that those who govern our own country are capable of doing what the foregoing account suggests they did?

The answer to that question, it seems entirely clear, is yes. To begin with, the leaders of many countries have shown themselves capable, throughout history, of grossly deceiving themselves about the likely consequences of their decisions; and America's leaders have been no exception. There is ample evidence of this latter fact: the Bay of Pigs invasion; the Carter Administration's ill-fated attempt to rescue American hostages from captivity in Teheran; the Korean War decision to cross the 38th parallel and advance to China's Manchurian border, ignoring clear warnings that the Chinese would intervene; the Johnson Administration's decision to bomb North Vietnam—in the belief that North Vietnam, instead of fighting back, would be quickly induced to capitulate.

Also recall what happened when, in 1978, there had been an earlier intrusion by a KAL airliner into Soviet strategic airspace. The airliner had penetrated at least 150 miles into Russian airspace before it was even fired upon by a Soviet jet fighter; it had then flown many miles farther, finally coming to an emergency landing with "only" two passengers killed. Against this background, it would not have been difficult for American intelligence officers to imagine that a repeat performance could also be pulled off "successfully." Indeed, the time spent by Flight 007 in Soviet airspace would actually be much less, and there would be a plausible destination at the end of the journey. Evidently abetted by the RC-135 which "happened" to be in the vicinity, Flight 007 in fact managed to overfly Kamchatka without being intercepted. Up to this point, a calculation that such an overflight could be pulled off successfully would have been proved correct—although even at this stage there would surely have been considerable risk.

After overflying Kamchatka, the airliner would of course be flying safely through international airspace until the second stage of its mission—when it would be over the tip of southern

Sakhalin for only a few minutes before again gaining the safety of international airspace over the Sea of Japan. It would not have been too difficult to imagine, against the background of the 1978 experience, that that could be pulled off, too. The fatal flaw in the plan, of course, was that the Soviet air defenses had been forewarned by the Kamchatka overflight, had concluded that the intruding aircraft was an American reconnaissance plane, had tracked the aircraft as it flew toward the highly sensitive Soviet positions guarding La Perouse Strait, had been waiting for Flight 007 when it flew into Soviet airspace over southern Sakhalin, and, despite its evasive maneuvers, had easily shot it down. The flight had thus ended, not like the "successful" KAL overflight of 1978, but like the Bay of Pigs invasion and the Iranian hostage rescue operation. On the basis of past experience, there is surely no reason to assume that U.S. officials are incapable of making any such miscalculations.

Nor can there be much doubt that President Ronald Reagan learned soon afterwards what had happened—even as President Eisenhower had known, when the EC-130 was shot down over Russia in 1958, "exactly what had happened and why." Bernard and Eskelson tell us how the highest U.S. authorities would have been informed of the fate of an important intelligence mission:

> The RC-135 has a super-advanced, ultra-secure communications system which is linked to the most sophisticated communications network in the world. This system . . . permits the instantane-

ous reporting of tactical intelligence to the highest levels of the U.S. government, including the President, from any location in the world. A message intended for the President is designated as a "Critic" and is required to be in the President's hands no more than 10 minutes after the actual time of transmission, for instance, from an RC-135 orbiting over the Sea of Japan.[146]

Thus, even as President Reagan was denouncing the Soviets for their "appalling and wanton misdeed," demanding that Moscow accept full blame and pay damages, he very likely knew that Flight 007 had been on a U.S. intelligence mission. Angry charges of the kind made by Reagan, Secretary of State George P. Shultz and other Administration officials would have been in the interest of keeping all the blame focussed on those who are, by definition, "the bad guys"—a public perception which, as we have seen, served the Administration's cold war purposes enormously. Otherwise the U.S. officials involved, including those in charge, would themselves have had to accept much of the blame for having sent the airliner, and all those aboard, to their deaths. Yet, on all the evidence, this is what they did.

Those men have plainly done their best to cover up the American intelligence role in the KAL airliner incident—to achieve what the intelligence community calls "plausible deniability." That would account for: the initial pretense that the United States has no "real time" intelligence capabilities in the Sea of Okhotsk region; the subsequent efforts, when that transparent pretense began to fall apart, to minimize what U.S. intelligence could have learned; the attempt, when it was inadvertently disclosed that an RC-135 had been patrolling nearby just before Flight 007 overflew Kamchatka, to put as much time and distance as possible between the two aircraft; the editing of the taped transcripts to show what the Administration was trying to show, while withholding the rest; the failure to provide the ICAO with information which had not already appeared in the press; and the failure even to release the taped transcripts of communications between KAL Flight 007 and Japanese air traffic controllers.

The reason for this secrecy, and manipulation of information, is obvious. If all the pertinent facts had become publicly known, it would have undermined the case the Administration was trying to make and pointed straight to the complicity of U.S. intelligence in the KAL airliner's flight over Soviet strategic territories.

So, too, the FBI, acting on behalf of the National Security Agency, in February 1984 warned Bernard and Eskelson that they had "technically" violated U.S. espionage laws by writing about the operations of RC-135 aircraft in the *Denver Post*. The two men, now civilians, were told to check with NSA officials before making any further disclosures.[147] In fact, the article had given away no technical secrets. Its authors had written only about the basic capabilities and operating routines of RC-135 aircraft, of which the Soviets are doubtless fully aware. But in revealing what they did, Bernard and Eskelson had accused the Reagan Administration of "a major effort . . . to bewilder the public concerning the capabilities of the . . . RC-135 and, more importantly, the National Security Agency."[148] What the two men revealed pointed very strongly to U.S. knowledge of, and complicity in, KAL Flight 007's intrusion into Soviet strategic airspace. And that, quite plainly, was what worried NSA officials about their disclosures—and possible future disclosures by Bernard and Eskelson or anyone else with inside knowledge of what had taken place. Eskelson, speaking to a reporter, rightly concluded that, "They want to do a heavy prior restraint on the First Amendment."[149] This, too, was aimed at sustaining the evident cover-up.

13. WOULD OUR LEADERS RISK THE LIVES OF INNOCENT PEOPLE?

But are we to believe that American leaders are in fact capable of knowingly gambling with the lives of innocent people? This is surely one of the most important questions raised by the entire affair. The answer is that our national leaders have done so repeatedly when they thought they were playing for high stakes in the struggle against "the Communist enemy." And this, indeed, is the larger significance of the KAL airliner incident. Consider, for example, the following:

(1) During the 1950's the U.S. military establishment, necessarily with the approval of the highest civilian authorities, ordered several hundred thousand American servicemen to participate in atomic maneuvers. Subjected to dangerously high doses of radiation, many of those servicemen in later years became fatally ill with leukemia and other forms of cancer. The story of their experiences has been told by various men who participated in the atomic maneuvers— among them, Lieutenant Thomas H. Saffer of the Marine Corps and Sergeant Major Orville Kelly. Blanche Wiesen Cook, reviewing their

book, *Countdown Zero,* observed in conclusion: "This harrowing book—with its catalogue of official cruelty, dishonesty and contempt for life—underscores how unprepared we are for our entrance into the nuclear age."[150]

(2) In the fall of 1962, a massive American covert operation (Operation Mongoose) aimed at toppling Fidel Castro's government escalated towards its October target date for achieving that objective; in that context, the Soviets placed missiles in Cuba comparable to those the United States had already deployed in Turkey and Italy. Theodore Sorensen, a close adviser to President John F. Kennedy, wrote afterwards: "To be sure, these Cuban missiles alone, in view of all the other megatonnage the Soviets were capable of unleashing upon us, did not substantially alter the strategic balance in fact . . . But that balance would have been substantially altered *in appearance* [emphasis added]; and in matters of national will and world leadership, as the President said later, such appearances contribute to reality."[151]

Hence the blockade and the crisis, with Attorney General Robert F. Kennedy eventually submitting Washington's final terms for a settlement in the form of an ultimatum. Orders were then issued for U.S. forces to prepare for an invasion of Cuba. As Robert Kennedy wrote, there was "a hope, not an expectation" that Khrushchev would revise his course "within the next few hours . . . The expectation was a military confrontation by Tuesday and possibly tomorrow."[152]

Robert Kennedy's own account of the Cuban missile crisis, *Thirteen Days,* had originally appeared with the apt subtitle, *The Story About How the World Almost Ended*. The sober-minded British journalist, Henry Fairlie, wrote of this episode:

> The question remains: What if Nikita Khrushchev had not backed down, not before the first step in the escalation of responses which had been planned, not before the second, not before the third, not until the final stage of ultimate thermonuclear war had been reached? The men, cool, rational, laconic and contained, whom [John F. Kennedy] had gathered to his service, planned for thirteen days a strategy of which the accepted end, if the Soviet Union did not react as they wished, was that they would burn the world to a cinder.[153]

This had been for the sake of removing missiles which had altered the strategic balance more "in appearance" than in reality.

(3) In August 1980, President Jimmy Carter signed Presidential Directive 59; as noted by Bernard T. Feld, editor of the *Bulletin of Atomic Scientists*, the directive contemplated American use of nuclear weapons "in an entirely offensive mode in an attempt to destroy the Soviet nuclear forces before they can be used against us." Feld commented: "The Carter Administration's decision to adopt, under pressure from the Reagan candidacy, a strategy of fighting a nuclear war based on a so-called limited counterforce exchange raises the serious question of whether our leaders have taken leave of their senses . . . The truth is that a nuclear war between the superpowers will be the last world war for centuries to come, with the only victors the radiation-resistant cock-

roaches. To play with doctrines of a fightable nuclear war is the ultimate folly."[154]

In a speech delivered at the Naval War College, President Carter's Secretary of Defense, Harold Brown, himself acknowledged "the immense uncertainties involved in any use of nuclear weapons . . . We know that what might start as a supposedly controlled, limited strike could well—in my view would very likely—escalate to a full-scale nuclear war. Further, we know that even limited nuclear exchanges would involve immense casualties and destruction."[155] Despite this belief that a "limited strike" would "very likely" precipitate a nuclear holocaust, the decision to resort to such a "limited strike" if thought necessary in "defense" of threatened U.S. "vital interests" was allowed to stand.

(4) More recently, as we have already seen, the Reagan Administration's "1984–1988 Defense Guidance" called for the adoption of a nuclear war strategy aimed at "decapitating" the Soviet state. As Arthur Macy Cox observed, "That means deploying nuclear weapons so accurate, so powerful and so fast on target that they could destroy the Soviet civilian and military leadership even in underground bunkers protected by stone and steel. They would also be able to destroy Soviet communications systems that control the ability to launch nuclear weapons . . . When we have deployed the first-strike weapons capable of 'decapitating' the Soviet state we will have the theoretical possibility of launching a surprise attack and 'winning' a nuclear war."[156]

The "decapitation" strategy adopted by the

Reagan Administration reflects the ideas of Colin Gray, Director of Strategic Studies at the Hudson Institute and adviser to the Pentagon under that Administration. The underlying concept, as expressed by Gray and co-author Keith Payne in an article entitled, "Victory is Possible," is that the United States should adopt an "intelligent . . . offensive strategy" in which a mere 20 million Americans would die—but with the United States emerging the "victor" with the "destruction of Soviet political authority and the emergence of a postwar world order compatible with Western values."[157]

PART THREE:
THE
POSSIBILITIES

14. THE IMPLICATIONS OF KAL FLIGHT 007—AND THE LESSONS

What do the several cases described above have to do with the immediate issue at hand—the question of whether or not our national leaders would gamble with the lives of innocent airline passengers in order to carry out an intelligence operation? Everything, it seems to me. The cases just cited not only demonstrate an obvious willingness by our national leaders to gamble, in one situation after another, with the lives of innocent people. What we have also seen is a willingness on their part, by no means the aberration of one on two "crazy" officials, to risk the survival of humanity itself in pursuit of their "national security" objectives. Are we really to believe that the same men would not dream of taking risks, for "compelling reasons of state," with the lives of airline passengers? The burden of proof surely does not lie with those who might argue that this is very probably what they in fact did.

With regard to the immediate issue at hand, we are left with this question: Congress, the courts, and the American people judged the Watergate break-in, a politically motivated burglary, to be legally and morally intolerable behavior by those in power, and those responsible for it were thrown out of office: indeed, some of them were sent to prison. How, then, will we deal with the strong possibility—rather, the likelihood—that government officials have used civilian airliners for dangerous intelligence missions, most recently with fatal results for 246 innocent passengers?

That is the legal and moral aspect of the matter. But the two KAL airliner incidents raise serious political issues as well. When Paul Warnke, Director of the Arms Control and Disarmament Agency under President Jimmy Carter, came during the summer of 1983 to speak at Syracuse University, where I teach, he observed that something always seems to pop up to disrupt attempts to end the nuclear arms race. Not all of these incidents, certainly, have been American intelligence operations. But many of them, coming at crucial moments, have obviously or quite evidently been such operations. Notably, there was Francis Gary Powers' ill-fated U-2 flight over the Soviet Union just before the Berlin summit conference. Retired Air Force Colonel L. Fletcher Prouty, who served for nine years as a Pentagon liaison officer with the C.I.A. for "special operations," wrote afterwards that, "every top official in the Government knew how important the summit conference was to the President." Also, "All of the regular launch authorities certainly knew that they were under strictest orders to do nothing that would jeopardize the success of the conferences."[158] Yet someone with the authority to do so ordered the flight.

Powers' U-2 was brought down, of course, by the Soviets; and when Nikita Khrushchev first disclosed that an American plane had been downed over Russia, "it began to look," as Prouty wrote, "as though the barbaric Russians were being trigger-happy again and that they had shot down another innocent weather plane."[159] But Khrushchev subsequently disclosed that Powers was in Soviet hands, it became clear that he had been on an intelligence mission, and in the ensuing furor the summit conference was wrecked. "With this great disaster," wrote Prouty, "the fifteen year search for a peaceful settlement in a world menaced by the atomic bomb came to an end."[160]

Then, in 1978, there had been the KAL airliner which "accidentally" flew over the Murmansk region of the Soviet Union at precisely the moment when Secretary of State Cyrus Vance was in Moscow for disarmament talks with the Soviet leaders. Again, the question: could those who evidently planned that flight have been unaware of the likelihood that it would eventually be brought down, perhaps creating an uproar as great as that caused by the U-2 incident, and that this would likely wreck any progress toward disarmament?

There was also, in 1979, the sudden "discovery" by U.S. intelligence of a Soviet "combat brigade" in Cuba, which aroused a furor in Congress soon after the Carter Administration sent the SALT II treaty to the U.S. Senate for approval. It later became evident that the "combat brigade" had no offensive capabilities at all and had been in Cuba ever since 1962. But the episode, together with the Soviet intervention in Afghanistan, so poisoned the political atmosphere that President Jimmy Carter asked the Senate to "delay consideration" of the treaty—a "delay" which has become semi-permanent.

Then we had KAL Flight 007's "accidental straying" over Soviet strategic positions in the Sea of Okhotsk region and the ensuing disaster—just as the momentous struggles over Pershing II and cruise missile deployment, and over the MX missile, were coming to a head. This raises the question: could the men who evidently planned Flight 007's penetration of Soviet strategic airspace, at this precise moment, have failed to know that it would probably cause an incident of some sort—and that this could tip the scales against those committed to ending the nuclear arms race?

Almost unbelievably, KAL Flight 007's venture into Soviet strategic airspace didn't end "accidental strayings" of this sort. On September 29, 1984, the Norwegians detected an aircraft crossing their northern border on a course taking it straight towards the Soviet Union's Kola Peninsula. The Norwegians scrambled two jet fighters and intercepted the plane when it was "within 15 minutes of straying over a heavily guarded Soviet naval base"—doubtless the Murmansk-Severomorsk complex. Had the aircraft not been turned back, observed a Norwegian Defense Ministry spokesman, "The consequences could have been serious."[161]

The straying aircraft proved to be an airliner operated by South Pacific Island Airways, on its way from Anchorage to Amsterdam carrying 120 Fiji troops bound for Middle East peace-keeping duties. The pilot, explaining his actions, claimed that the airliner's radar had been faulty and that, before the jets reached his aircraft, he had realized that he was 500 miles off course and turned westward. But the Norwegian Defense Ministry stated that their fighter planes had intercepted the straying aircraft.[162]

When asked about the incident, a representative of South Pacific Island Airways said in Honolulu that its service was limited to the South Pacific and that the airline made no flights to Amsterdam.[163] Moreover, the U.S. Federal Aviation Administration stated afterwards that the airline had violated its operating rights by flying over the polar route—designated as "minimum navigational performance airspace" requiring special navigational skills or equipment. Said the F.A.A.: "S.P.I.A. did not meet this requirement and was not authorized to make the flight."[164] The circumstances surrounding this episode, too, were highly suspicions. And we are again left with the question: could it have been purely coincidental that this unauthorized flight had "strayed" off course in precisely the direction, out of all those in which it might have gone, which would have taken it over the same Soviet naval base KAL Flight 902 had "strayed" over in April 1978?

This pattern of events points to a sinister possibility—that the sub rosa forces created by our national leaders to prosecute the cold war have often been able, at decisive moments, to thwart open processes which might have led us toward peace. What we must ask ourselves is whether we are willing to be dragged down the road toward a nuclear holocaust in this fashion—and if not, what we must do at this crucial moment in history to ensure that we, the threatened peoples, will in fact be able to determine our own fate.

The methods employed by those to whom our lives have been entrusted is not the only issue. The most serious question is where we perceive them to be leading us and what, if anything, must be done about it. Clearly, what made it hard to believe that our leaders would gamble with the lives of airline passengers in an intelligence operation was the fact that the results of that evident gamble became a horrible, undeniable reality. But it is even plainer that those same men are prepared to gamble with the survival of humankind itself. They have told us quite openly what they are prepared to do "if necessary," and even now are urging us to prepare for that eventuality by arming ourselves with shovels for a projected mass exodus to the countryside—so that we and our families might cower there in the holes we dig while a "protracted" nuclear war, more likely the final holocaust, rages overhead. Since the unspeakable horror of such a holocaust has not descended upon us yet, many of us resist accepting the fact that our "leaders" would ever permit such a thing to happen—much less cause it to happen because of the course of action upon which they are embarked. The very thought is intolerable.

But the tragic affair of KAL Flight 007 has

come to us, it seems to me, as a warning. Assuming that my analysis of the affair is correct, does it not tell us something about the dangerous lengths to which our "national security" managers will go in their preparations to "fight and win" a nuclear war? Are we not all passengers on a flight piloted by reckless gamblers? Have those men not been flying us, without regard for the perils which lie so plainly ahead, on a course leading straight towards catastrophe?

It is not that these men *intend* to lead the nation, and the world, into nuclear war. Rather, it is that they can conceive of no way to "preserve peace," in the face of what they conceive to be an unrelenting "enemy," other than to prepare for nuclear war. Hence this revealing exchange between Secretary of Defense Caspar Weinberger and a Harvard student:

> Harvard student: Do you believe the world is going to end, and, if you do, do you think it will be by an act of God or an act of men?
>
> Weinberger: I have read the Book of Revelation and, yes, I believe the world is going to end—by an act of God, I hope—but every day I think that time is running out.
>
> Harvard student: Are you scared?
>
> Weinberger: I worry that we will not have enough time to get strong enough to prevent war. I think of World War II and how long it took to prepare for it, to convince people that rearmament for war was needed. I fear we will not be ready. I think time is running out . . . but I have faith.[165]

Hence, also, the Reagan Administration's expressed determination to create capabilities for "prevailing" even in a "protracted" nuclear war "should deterrence fail."

If ever there was a self-fulfilling prophesy with ominous implications, this is surely it. For the determination to develop and deploy a vast array of first-strike weaponry, so that the Soviet Union can be "decapitated" if the crunch ever comes, leaves the Soviet Union with no alternative except to make strenuous efforts to "keep up" with the United States. Inevitably, this will take the form of developing first-strike weapon systems to match those deployed by the United States—with both sides then finding it necessary to place their nuclear forces on a computerized, launch-on-warning status. As Paul Warnke and others have pointed out, the question of whether or not humanity is to be plunged into a nuclear abyss would then come to rest on "hair trigger" judgements by these entirely fallible computerized systems in a time of grave international crisis.

Nor is there much doubt that such a crisis, unless the current trend is reversed, would inevitably come. For the Reagan Administration's determination to create nuclear war-fighting capabilities has been combined, as we have seen, with a confrontationist strategy—that of conducting a "full court press" against the Soviet Union. Unless abandoned, these two elements together are certain to produce an intensification of the hostility and fear on both sides; and this will almost certainly culminate, sooner or later, in the "crunch" where it will become necessary to "get them before they get us." The fantasies of "victory" entertained by our "national security" managers plainly rest on the desperate gamble that when that moment comes, we will be able to "beat the Russians to the punch." The Reagan Administration's "Defense Guidance" would have us preparing ourselves for a final "High Noon" scenario—with everything being gambled on which nuclear gunslinger has the "fastest draw."

But those nuclear gunslingers aren't out there in the street all by themselves, with nobody's lives but their own at stake. It obviously isn't six-shooters on which their trigger fingers rest. And there won't be any "winners" and "losers" in the "High Noon" showdown for which our leaders are preparing us. Whoever pushes the button first will not only, as he might imagine, be "taking care of the enemy once and for all." He will be committing the act by which much or all of humanity will be engulfed in a final, apocalyptic orgy of mass murder-suicide. He will be committing the ultimate crime against life on earth.

And the rest of us? Our true situation, as suggested earlier, is exactly akin to that of the passengers who were flown to their deaths on KAL Flight 007. But the destination towards which we are being flown by those at the controls is absolutely clear—and we are not yet at the catastrophic end of our flight. Moreoever, nothing requires us to sit passively in our seats. We can turn the flight around.

15. WHAT SHOULD BE DONE?

What, then, should be done? The foregoing analysis of KAL Flight 007 and what it signifies leads us, in my own view, to four conclusions:

(1) *There should be a Congressional investigation of the affair; and, if the case presented here is proved correct, those responsible must be brought to account for their actions.*

What we have seen here, I think, is a strong *prima facie* case suggesting that U.S. Government officials have been guilty of serious wrong-doing—of wrong-doing which cost the lives of 269 people. The Reagan Administration itself cannot be expected to carry out the thorough investigation needed to bring out all the facts. Only Congress can do that; and it surely has the constitutional duty to do so—demanding all the records which have been withheld and addressing all the questions which have been raised here and in the press. If, having done so, they are able to provide us with a better explanation than the one presented here for all the acts of commission and omission by the various parties involved, the air will have been cleared once and for all. If, on the other hand, they find that the analysis presented here is essentially correct, they obviously have the duty to bring those responsible to account for their actions.

(2) *There needs to be a thorough Congressional review of intelligence operations of the kind discussed here.*

Again assuming that my analysis is correct, the KAL airliner incident also dramatizes the dangers inherent in aggressive intelligence operations of this kind. Recall that two NSA analysts had become so fearful that one such operation might spark World War III that, after failing in their attempt to alert Congress, they defected to the Soviet Union. George F. Kennan addressed himself to the same issue:

> One of the most dangerous aspects of these far-flung and extravagant efforts at snooping is that they, like many of the regular military preparations, reflect a pattern of assumptions in which the relationship between the two countries is virtually indistinguishable from what would prevail if a state of war already existed or if the early coming-into-existence of such a state of war was regarded as inevitable. But such assumptions, once made the basis for governmental activity on an extensive scale, soon come to take on reality in the minds of those who are called upon to act on the basis of them; and they then have a contagious effect—both on the remainder of the governmental establishment within which they operate and on the one against which they are directed.

Kennan also pointed to a second danger inherent in such activities—the great difficulty of controlling and adjusting them to the needs of a constructive relationship.[166]

Under the American Constitution, it is Con-

gress which has the power to declare war—
meaning, to make the ultimate decision as to
whether or not the nation will go to war. But this
power, and responsibility, will surely be proved
utterly meaningless in the nuclear age unless
Congress asserts its authority over processes
which could easily lead us into a nuclear
holocaust. And what this clearly suggests is the
need for a thorough Congressional review of
U.S. intelligence operations with a view to curb-
ing those provocative operations which are not
essential for strictly defensive purposes. To place
the problem in proper perspective, it would be
helpful to imagine the kind of situation which
would surely arise if Soviet aircraft based just beyond our borders—say, on Cuba—made it a
regular practice to penetrate U.S. airspace for the
purpose of activating U.S. air defense systems;
and if, besides, Soviet naval forces made it a practice to conduct maneuvers just off our shores.

(3) *Initiatives must be undertaken to reverse the nuclear arms race and normalize relations with the Soviet
Union.*

The continued escalation of the nuclear arms
race, and of bitter enmity between the United
States and the Soviet Union, is completely un-
necessary—even as it is insanely dangerous. But
to find our way out of this terrible bind, we must
understand the basic process by which we and
the Russians, together with the rest of humankind, have been brought to the point of extreme
peril in which we find ourselves. That process
can be quite simply stated: when one of the nuclear superpowers has built up its nuclear arse-

nal, the other has felt threatened—and has responded with a matching effort which has increased the first superpower's sense of insecurity. And this, in turn, has produced renewed efforts by that first superpower to "catch up" or "regain superiority." Thus, the nuclear arms race has escalated from each stage to a still more dangerous one, in an endless action-reaction process which has led not to increased security for either superpower but to ever increasing danger to both the United States and the Soviet Union.

It is also this action-reaction process which keeps the United States and the Soviet Union politically and psychologically committed to a course which, in the end, can only prove suicidal for the peoples of both countries. For each superpower's actions produce the reactions by the other which reinforce the belief of its adversary, leaders and citizens alike, that the other side is "out to get us" and that renewed "defensive measures" are necessary. A constant feature of this process has been the blaming of the other superpower. But doing so—in our case, blaming the Soviets—obviously does not solve the problem. It does not, and cannot, get us off the mutually suicidal course upon which we and the Russians find ourselves. Indeed, the accusations and counter-accusations which have become such a prominent feature of the deteriorating U.S.-Soviet relationship have only had the effect of intensifying the fear and hostility underlying the nuclear arms race.

Clearly, the choice confronting the United

States is whether we should continue this deadly competition in nuclear armaments or whether we should strive to end it altogether. It is not likely that a Reagan Administration committed, as Tom Wicker wrote, to "an unrelenting war to the death" with the Soviet Union will know how to end the arms race and normalize relations with that country. And yet, there is very little doubt that those objectives can in fact be achieved.

The dramatic transformation of America's relationship with Communist China, after years of bitter hostility, suggests how this can be done. Let us recall for a moment the main features of that relationship and how it was changed.

For more than two decades, it will be remembered, the U.S. Government perceived "Red China" to be no less an international "menace" than the Soviet Union, requiring China's exclusion from the family of nations, a total economic embargo, and unrelenting military "containment" of China's presumed aggressive tendencies. America's policy towards the "Chinese Communist enemy" went farther even than that. The essence of U.S. policy during the Eisenhower Administration was conveyed to a Congressional committee in January 1954, by Walter S. Robertson, Assistant Secretary of State for Far Eastern Affairs. After an off-the-record discussion, Robertson confirmed this summary of his own remarks by Congressman Coudert:

> The heart of the present policy toward China and Formosa is that there is to be kept alive a constant threat of military action vis-a-vis Red

China in the hope that at some point there will be an internal breakdown . . .

In other words, a cold war waged under the leadership of the United States, with constant threat of attack against Red China, led by Formosa and other Far Eastern groups and militarily supported by the United States.[167]

In other words, the Eisenhower Administration, with Secretary of State John Foster Dulles at the foreign policy helm, was committed to an "unrelenting war" against Communist China virtually identical in spirit to the anti-Soviet crusade contemplated by the Reagan Administration's five-year "Defense Guidance."

The perception of Communist China as a "menace to the world" which had to be contained militarily persisted through both the Kennedy and Johnson administrations. Indeed, both of them came to perceive China, not the Soviet Union, as America's "main enemy." President John F. Kennedy, commenting to the press on the likelihood that China would soon have nuclear weapons, stated in August 1963: "I would regard that combination of weak countries around it, seven hundred million people, a Stalinist regime, and nuclear powers, and a government *determined on war* [emphasis added] as a means of bringing about its ultimate success, as potentially a more dangerous situation than any we faced since the end of the Second (World) War."[168] Amplifying on such views a month after Kennedy's assassination, Assistant Secretary of State Roger Hilsman asserted that whereas the Soviet Union was willing to recognize certain common interests shared by mankind, "notably survival," China was not.[169]

So, too, the Johnson Administration, which imagined China to be the ultimate source of "Communist aggression" in Vietnam. Thus President Lyndon B. Johnson, speaking on April 7, 1965: "Over this war—and all Asia—is another reality: the deepening shadow of Communist China. The rulers in Hanoi are urged on by Peking . . ."[170] With China viewed in this way, the *Wall Street Journal* had a month earlier reported the existence of "vastly detailed" plans to "return China to the dark ages" if necessary. The United States would probably start by bombing along China's "supply lines all the way back to the home-front factories," and could "plaster almost at will such targets as petroleum and ammunitions dumps, air fields, rail hubs and bridges . . . nuclear bombs would also be available if the President decided to use them."[171]

The Soviets were then viewed, and treated, very differently. The Johnson Administration's belief, as reported by the *New York Times* shortly after the U.S. began bombing North Vietnam, was "that there is, or ought to be, a general coincidence of Soviet and American interests in Asia, at least to the extent that each wishes to contain Chinese influence among Asian Communists and the region's non-Communist nations." With regard to the U.S. bombing offensive, American officials "went to great lengths to explain their actions to the Soviet Government. They underlined assurances that they desired to avoid wider war and that they appreciated the Russians' dilemma."[172] In other words, the Soviet Union was then perceived to be basically a "friend" in the common task of containing the "aggressive tendencies" of what was then viewed as the "main enemy"—Communist China.

Not surprisingly, the Chinese Communists responded with considerable verbal belligerence to such manifestations of America's "containment" policy in Asia—as in Lin Piao's September 1965 characterization of the United States as "the most rabid aggressor in human history and the most ferocious common enemy of the people of the world."[173] Such denunciations, in their turn, strongly reinforced the conviction among American policymakers that the "ChiComs," as they were called back in those days, were "out to get us." Indeed, it was then common for U.S. official spokesmen to evoke images of "Munich" in warning against "appeasement" of Communist China. There is no doubt that America's policy-makers of that era believed fervently in these images of an "evil" Communist China bent on a Hitler-like policy of armed conquest—just as the nation's policy-makers of more recent times, especially those of the Reagan Administration, are convinced of the "necessity" for arming America to the teeth, with both conventional and nuclear weapons, for relentless struggle to contain "Soviet aggression."

It was against this background of bitterly hostile U.S.-Chinese relations that President Richard M. Nixon undertook in 1972 to normalize relations with this very same "Red China"—at a time when U.S. ground forces were being withdrawn from a losing effort in Vietnam to combat what our policy-makers had thought to be "aggression" largely inspired by the "ChiComs." Nixon's initiative, highlighted by television footage of a beaming Nixon shaking hands with Mao Zedong in Peking, was nonetheless hailed as a great foreign policy triumph; and the intense mutual hostility and fear which had brought the United States and China several times (after Korea) to the brink of war evaporated virtually overnight.

But Washington's belief that the United States was beset by a powerful "Communist enemy" did not disappear; the focus of those fears merely shifted to the Soviet Union. Yesterday's "friend" against China suddenly became the "main enemy," and in this context our policy-makers began to "play the China card" against the Russians. President Jimmy Carter's national security adviser, Zbigniew Brzezinski, ventured to Peking in May 1978 to explore the possibilities for U.S.-Chinese cooperation to "contain" the Soviet Union. He was followed there by Secretary of Defense Harold Brown in January 1980; and in May 1980 the Chinese Defense Minister, Geng Biao, would be found touring American military installations and defense industries. These several trips produced "high-level military cooperation," including the establishment of an American electronic surveillance station in China to monitor Soviet missile tests.[174]

The Reagan Administration followed in the Carter Administration's tracks. In June 1981, shortly after President Ronald Reagan took office, Secretary of State Alexander Haig visited Peking, where he announced that China would be eligible to buy American arms. Nothing came of it at the time, apparently because of Peking's unhappiness over the Reagan Administration's arms sales to Taiwan. But in February 1983, the United States and China agreed on steps to restore high-level military contacts between the two countries. Meeting in Peking with Secretary of State George Shultz, Haig's successor, Chinese Foreign Minister Zhang Aiping "agreed with an American suggestion for closer military relations and with procedures that United States officials hope will lead to an early visit to China by Secretary of Defense Caspar Weinberger."[175] No longer is there any talk in Washington of the "China menace" or of the need for massive military efforts to "contain Chinese aggression."

Lest it be thought that all this is a digression, allow me to suggest that it is not—that, indeed, it gets to the heart of the problem. KAL Flight 007's flight over Soviet strategic territories, assuming my analysis to be correct, was both an act in the struggle against the (Soviet) "Communist enemy" and an event which reinforced American perceptions of Russia's "evil nature"—thus leading to an intensification of the struggle. The basic problem, of which the KAL airliner incident was but a symptom, is how to transform the U.S.-Soviet relationship into one that is safe for the peoples of both countries and for humanity at large. I have dwelt at some length on the U.S.-

China relationship, including the dramatic transformation it underwent, because there is much to
be learned from it.

To begin with, it became entirely evident that
the Chinese Communist government's hostility
towards the United States had not in fact been
the expression of a presumed ideological impera-
tive to "take over Asia" or, eventually, to "destroy
America." Rather, it had been very largely the
response to an avowedly hostile American policy
which expressed itself in efforts, all along China's
periphery, to "contain" that country militarily;
also, in periodic threats to attack China itself. Before President Nixon's initiative, as former National Security Council staffer Roger Morris
wrote, American diplomacy "had been impotent
to surmount its own mindless posture of belligerence in Asia."[176] When Nixon abandoned that
"mindless posture of belligerence" and extended
the hand of reconciliation to Mao Zedong, the
Chinese abandoned their own "hostile attitude"
towards the United States. As a result, Americans
began to *see* China in an entirely different way
and the perceived need to "contain" an "aggressive China" simply vanished.

The manner in which Nixon set this process in
motion is also highly instructive. Whereas it had
previously been thought necessary to threaten
China with superior force in order to curb
China's presumed "aggressive intentions," Nixon
carried out a series of *conciliatory* actions aimed at
sending very different signals about *America's own*
intentions. He eased restrictions on trade with

and travel to China, withdrew the Seventh Fleet from the Formosa Strait, and halted U-2 reconnaissance flights over China. These were all unilateral initiatives which could be undertaken without in any way jeopardizing American security; and they obviously had the desired effect of convincing the Chinese that the United States genuinely wanted improved relations between the two countries. Mao Zedong reciprocated by inviting Nixon to Peking and, as they say, the rest is history.

Would the Soviets respond in like manner to conciliatory initiatives of this sort? There are very good reasons for thinking that they would. When there have been conciliatory gestures from the United States, the Soviets have been responsive in the past. We have, for example, this characterization by Edward Crankshaw of Nikita Khrushchev's reaction when, in 1959, he was invited to meet with President Dwight D. Eisenhower at Camp David, Maryland:

> It is impossible to exaggerate the climacteric importance of this event in Khrushchev's eyes. Time and again he had angled for the invitation, laying himself open to snubs of a kind which no other statesman in the world would have dared to risk. But from his point of view it was worth it. When President Eisenhower's invitation at last came, it established the Soviet Union for all the world to see as the acknowledged equal to the United States of America; it established Khrushchev personally at home as the man who could work miracles; it gave him the chance of presenting himself to the world as the one man who could save the peace. The Moscow press was beside itself with

exultation. It spoke recklessly of the coming visit
as marking an historical "turning point" and the
beginning of a new age.[177]

Upon returning to Moscow from Camp David,
Khrushchev praised Eisenhower as a man of
peace—at the time causing "outraged incredul-
ity" in Peking.[178] As we know, this promising beginning was to have been followed in the spring
of 1960 by a Berlin summit conference called to
settle outstanding European issues and to lay
solid foundations for peaceful U.S.-Soviet relations. As we also know, these moves toward peace
collapsed in the furor following Francis Gary
Powers' ill-fated U-2 flight across the Soviet Union in April 1960.

During the final year of his presidency, John F.
Kennedy would also make a break, in his famous
American University speech of June 10, 1963,
with America's past policies toward the Soviet
Union. "The President was determined," wrote
Theodore Sorenson, "to put a fundamentally
new emphasis on the peaceful and the positive in
our relations with the Soviets. He did not want
that new policy diluted by the usual threats of
destruction, boasts of nuclear stockpiles and lec-
tures on Soviet treachery."[179] In his speech, Kennedy therefore called upon the American people
to "re-examine our attitude toward the Soviet
Union." Both the United States and the Soviet
Union "have a mutually deep interest," he
affirmed, "in a just and genuine peace and in
halting the arms race . . . So, let us not be blind to
our differences—but let us also direct attention
to our common interests and to the means by

which those differences can be resolved."[180] Having said these things, Kennedy announced that negotiations would soon take place in Moscow to seek agreement on a comprehensive nuclear test ban; and he took the further step, to "make clear our good faith and solemn convictions on the matter," of declaring that the United States would not conduct nuclear tests in the atmosphere so long as other countries also refrained from doing so.

Richard J. Barnet has very well summarized the Russian reaction to Kennedy's speech:

> Soviet citizens found it electrifying. For months some carried clippings of it in their wallets. It was an appeal for an end to the cold war, the first speech by an American President in more than a decade and a half to mention that the people of the Soviet Union were human beings and to pay tribute to their bravery and suffering in the war. It marked the first official attempt to exorcise the devil theory that determined official attitudes and public opinion towards the Soviet Union.[181]

Khrushchev himself told Averell Harriman, the chief American negotiator at the nuclear test ban talks in Moscow, that Kennedy's address had been "the greatest speech by an American President since Roosevelt."[182] The Soviets suspended their own atmospheric nuclear tests in response to Kennedy's unilateral initiative; and on July 25, a mere six weeks after Kennedy's American University speech, a treaty banning atmospheric tests was signed in Moscow.

As we know, continued underground testing was permitted by the treaty. Kennedy, confronted by Pentagon demands for "the conduct of comprehensive, aggressive, and continuous underground test programs,"[183] had been reluctant to press for a total test ban. So the arms race continued; and the momentum towards peace which had been set in motion by Kennedy's speech was arrested when, on November 22, President Kennedy was assassinated.

Yet the episode made clear Moscow's desire to end the arms race and normalize relations with the United States, and its readiness to respond to American initiatives which had those ends in view. Indeed, for the sake of these ends, the Soviets had then been prepared to concede nuclear superiority to the United States. Khrushchev, writing to Kennedy in December 1962, had suggested "that the time has come now to put an end once and for all to nuclear tests"— even though the United States enjoyed a very substantial lead over the Soviet Union in nuclear weaponry. The partial test ban treaty agreed to by the Soviets was also advantageous to the United States. As Secretary of Defense Robert McNamara told the U.S. Senate, the United States had "substantially more experience" in underground testing and would therefore be permitted under the treaty to "prolong the duration of our technological superiority."[184]

During the post-Kennedy, post-Khrushchev era, President Richard Nixon resumed the effort to normalize relations with the Soviet Union in negotiations with Leonid Brezhnev; the result was a series of agreements which collectively formed the basis for "detente." The movement in that direction did not last long. Although the concept of "detente" was accorded great importance within the Soviet Union, the retreat from it in the United States began during the Ford Administration—under pressure from Ronald Reagan's looming presidential candidacy. When Reagan became President, the idea of "detente" was replaced completely by a commitment to unrelenting struggle against what he himself, and quite obviously his chief advisers, perceive to be an "evil empire."

The Soviets, for their part, have suggested that they still strongly desire an end to the nuclear arms race and to the Cold War itself. Thomas Powers has provided the following summary, based on conversations with Soviet officials, of the direction in which they say they would like to go:

> They cite the numerous public statements of Brezhnev and Andropov calling for peace and arms control, offering to reduce Soviet missiles targeted on Europe to 162 (the number of French and British missiles), pledging "no first use" of nuclear weapons in the event of war, accepting the principle of a freeze, proposing a general European nonaggression pact leading to outright dissolution of the NATO and Warsaw Pact treaties, suggesting a joint U.S.-Soviet study of space-based defense systems and a ban of same, urging serious talks in Vienna on mutual balanced-force reductions, and in general promising a readiness to negotiate an end to the arms race and the Cold War. They insist that Moscow is ready, that this isn't just talk . . . You don't believe us? The Russians say, *Try Us.*[185]

To take advantage of the opportunity which is evidently there, American diplomacy would have to be able to surmount a posture of belligerence as mindless as that with which it confronted Communist China before the time of Richard Nixon. There is little reason to believe that the Reagan Administration will be able to do so. During President Reagan's first term, his Administration rejected the concept of a bilateral nuclear weapons freeze. It refused to resume the adjourned comprehensive test ban negotiations, a resumption requested by British Prime Minister Margaret Thatcher's government as well as by the Soviets. And the Reagan Administration also rejected requests for negotiations to ban weapons from space—this so the United States can carry out a space warfare program aimed, in the words of Air Force Space Command planners, at restoring "preatomic notions of military superiority" and making "conflict at the upper levels of violence [nuclear attack] again thinkable."[186]

True, following President Reagan's reelection in November 1984, there is to be a resumption of U.S.-Soviet nuclear arms negotiations. But the Administration remains committed to its "Star Wars" program and, despite a budget deficit growing to dangerous proportions, to a continuing U.S. military build-up. There have been no indications that President Reagan himself has changed his basic outlook or that there is anything like a strong movement within his Administration calling for a *fundamental* change of approach toward U.S.-Soviet relations and the nuclear arms race. The general direction in which the Reagan Administration remains determined to go seems entirely clear.

And yet, the opportunity to make peace is evidently there if, as in Kennedy's brief moment of vision and Nixon's openings to both China and Russia, our leaders have both the imagination and will to seize that opportunity. An initiative in the same spirit would not solve at a single stroke all the accumulated problems of nearly four decades of Cold War. But the nuclear arms race can almost certainly be ended and relations with the Soviet Union normalized if that is the direction in which our political leaders truly wish to go. The achievement of those two ends would in turn create an atmosphere far more conducive to a resolution of other problems. It is by no means inconceivable that America's relationship with the Soviet Union can be transformed in the same way that the U.S.-China relationship was transformed. It isn't at all inconceivable that the Cold War can be ended, making it possible to shift vast human and economic resources to constructive purposes, and making the world a much safer place for all of its inhabitants.

(4) *The responsibility for ending the nuclear arms race lies finally with every one of us.*

I have made the foregoing suggestion about a means to end the arms race and normalize relations with the Soviet Union because the situation urgently demands that we turn away from the perilous course we are on; also, because I think that an approach to Russia based on Richard Nixon's approach to China would be a promising one. Nixon's approach, and John F. Kennedy's first steps toward detente with Russia, show that imaginative peace-making initiatives are not beyond the realm of what some political leaders have been able to do in their best moments.

But I am not so naive as to think, at this late

stage of the Cold War, that those in power are often persuaded to act by even the most compelling and rational arguments. In May 1981, on the occasion of being awarded the Albert Einstein Peace Prize, George F. Kennan spoke of this problem: "The danger is so obvious. So much has already been said. What is to be gained by reiteration? What good would it do now? Look at the record. Over all these years the competition has proceeded steadily, relentlessly, without the faintest regard for all these warning voices."[187]

For the most part, our political leaders have not been part of the solution; they have been a major part of the problem. It is idle to hope for a political miracle and foolish to leave our fate, and that of our children, in the hands of those who have generally given us little reason to believe that such trust is warranted. It was for good reason that President Dwight D. Eisenhower, although then "the most powerful man on earth," stated his conviction:

> Above all, the people. I like to believe that the people in the long run are going to do more to promote peace than our government. Indeed, I think the people want peace so much that one day the government had better get out of their way and let them have it.[188]

There was recognition here, perhaps a confession, that our "leaders" are not likely to make peace until the popular demand for it becomes overwhelming—surpassing in power the force of those influences which have thus far kept the U.S. Government harnessed to demands for endless struggle against "the enemy."

There is some reason to be optimistic about the possibilities. As we know from public opinion polls, the vast majority of the American people favor a bilateral nuclear weapons freeze as a first step toward reversing the arms race and ending the nuclear peril. The problem before us is to translate this sentiment into a "will of the people" which cannot be denied. We have a precedent for how this can be done. The anti-war movement of the 1960's finally reached such proportions that the President who had been prosecuting the Vietnam war, Lyndon B. Johnson, was forced to not seek re-election; and his successor—the same Richard Nixon who, in probably his best moment as President, made peace with China—finally found it impossible to continue the war.

What we must do today is entirely clear. As in the 1960's, we must not allow those in power to define, out of their own, "mindless belligerence," the political realities all of us face. We must remove from office those who can think of nothing to do except, in George Kennan's phrase, to pile "weapon upon weapon, missile upon missile, new levels of destructiveness upon old ones."[189] We must work to place in office men and women who are truly committed to ending the nuclear arms race. And we must create a political climate which will make it safe for politicians who are so inclined, in the face of denunciations from those committed to ceaseless struggle against "the enemy," to take initiatives for peace.

The situation we are in, if I might be allowed a final metaphor, is like that of people in a lifeboat struggling through stormy seas. Some are pulling at the oars as hard as they can. Others are rowing half-heartedly or are simply sitting in the boat. The problem is a simple one. If not enough people row, the lifeboat is almost certain to founder and sink in increasingly heavy seas, drowning all those aboard. But if enough people take up oars and put their backs into the task, we will have every reason to believe that our lifeboat will be able to make it safely to land. Edmund Burke put the problem well: "The only thing necessary for the triumph of evil is for good men [and women] to do nothing."

NOTES

1. New York Times, August 14, 1981.
2. New York Times, June 1, 1982.
3. CBS Evening News, Sept. 5, 1983.
4. New York Times, March 9, 1983.
5. New York Times, Aug. 31, 1984.
6. New York Times, September 6, 1983.
7. New York Times, Aug. 31, 1984.
8. New York Times, Aug. 31, 1984.
9. New York Times, September 3, 1983.
10. Washington Post, September 4, 1983.
11. New York Times, September 4, 1983.
12. The New Yorker, October 3, 1983.
13. New York Times, September 2, 1983.
14. Ibid.
15. New York Times, September 7, 1983.
16. New York Times, September 10, 1983.
17. New York Times, October 8, 1983.
18. San Francisco Examiner and Chronicle, September 4, 1983.
19. David Pearson, "K.A.L 007: What the U.S. Knew and When We Knew It," The Nation, Aug. 18–25, 1984.
20. Report cited by Antony Verney in a letter to the editor, Manchester Guardian Weekly, September 18, 1983.
21. Washington Post, September 4, 1983.
22. Miami Herald, September 11, 1983.
23. Ibid.
24. New York Times, September 10, 1983.
25. Manchester Guardian Weekly, September 18, 1983.
26. New York Times, September 8, 1983.
27. San Francisco Examiner and Chronicle, September 4, 1983.
28. New York Times, September 2, 1983.
29. Ibid.
30. James Bamford. The Puzzle Palace (Middlesex, England: Penguin Books edition, 1983), pp. 233–234.
31. Ibid., p. 181.
32. Ibid., pp. 235–238.

33. Ibid., p. 183.
34. Ibid., pp. 183–184.
35. Ibid., p. 208
36. George Wilson, Washington Post, September 2, 1983.
37. New York Times, September 5, 1983.
38. Washington Post, September 5, 1983.
39. New York Times, September 10, 1983.
40. New York Times, October 7, 1983.
41. Pearson, *op. cit.*
42. Ibid.
43. Washington Post, September 7, 1983.
44. New York Times, October 7, 1983.
45. Denver Post, September 13, 1983.
46. New York Times, September 14, 1983.
47. Ibid.
48. Washington Post, September 2, 1983.
49. Washington Post, September 11, 1983.
50. New York Times, September 5, 1983.
51. New York Times, September 7, 1983.
52. New York Times, September 10, 1983.
53. As reported in the New York Times, September 14, 1983.
54. Denver Post, September 13, 1983.
55. International Civil Aviation Organization, "Summary of Findings and Conclusions," December 1983. All references to ICAO findings are from this report and the ICAO press release dated December 13, 1983.
56. ICAO, "Summary of Findings and Conclusions."
57. San Francisco Examiner and Chronicle, September 4, 1983.
58. Ibid.
59. Ibid.
60. New York Times, September 11, 1983. Also see Dr. Rudolph Braunberg, a former Lufthansa pilot, in "Die Toten und die Vermarktung der Trauer," Deutsches Allgemeines Sonntagsblatt. From translated excerpts in Counterspy, December 1983–February 1984. Wrote Braunberg: "It is possible that the pilot made a mistake during the input process, but whatever he does is checked by two other people—the co-pilot and flight engineer."
61. San Francisco Examiner and Chronicle, September 4, 1983.
62. Ibid.
63. New York Times, November 17, 1983.
64. Ibid.
65. San Francisco Examiner and Chronicle, September 4, 1983.
66. Braunberg, op. cit.

67. New York Times, September 11, 1983.

68. Pearson, op. cit.

69. New York Times, May 30, 1982.

70. *Evaluation of Fiscal Year 1979 Arms Control Impact Statements: Toward More Informed Congressional Participation in National Security Policy-Making*, a report prepared for the House International Relations Committee by the Foreign Affairs and National Defense Division of the Congressional Research Service of the Library of Congress (January 3, 1979), p. 119.

71. Robert C. Aldridge. *The Counterforce Syndrome* (Washington, D.C.: Institute for Policy Studies, 1978), pp. 45–55.

72. Thomas B. Allen and Norman Polmar, "The Silent Chase," New York Times Magazine, January 1, 1984.

73. Ibid.

74. New York Times, September 6, 1983.

75. Allen and Polmar, op. cit.

76. New York Times, September 4, 1983.

77. Michael Klare, "Asia: Theater of Nuclear War," *South*, November 1983.

78. New York Times, September 2, 1983.

79. Klare, op. cit.

80. Ibid.

81. Aviation Week and Space Technology, February 28, 1983.

82. Klare, op. cit.

83. Syracuse Herald-American, April 18, 1982.

84. Robert Scheer. *With Enough Shovels* (New York: Vintage Books, 1983), p. 7.

85. New York Times, September 2, 1983.

86. Washington Post, July 11, 1976.

87. Miami Herald, September 11, 1983.

88. San Francisco Examiner and Chronicle, September 4, 1983.

89. Armed Forces Journal, May 1981.

90. San Francisco Examiner and Chronicle, September 4, 1983.

91. Miami Herald, September 11, 1983.

92. Quoted by Fred Kaplan, Boston Globe, September 19, 1983.

93. Boston Globe, September 19, 1983

94. Miami Herald, September 11, 1983.

95. Washington Post, July 11, 1976.

96. Boston Globe, September 19, 1983.

97. San Francisco Examiner and Chronicle, September 4, 1983.

98. Boston Globe, September 19, 1983.

99. New York Times, April 23, 1978.

100. New York Times, April 22, 1978.

101. New York Times, April 21, 1978.
102. New York Times, April 22, 1978.
103. New York Times, April 23, 1978.
104. Washington Post, September 2, 1983.
105. Kevin Close, Washington Post, September 4, 1983.
106. New York Times, April 22, 1978.
107. Ibid.
108. Pearson, op. cit.
109. Washington Post, September 4, 1983.
110. New York Times, April 22, 1978.
111. Washington Post, April 23, 1978.
112. Washington Post, April 24, 1978.
113. New York Times, April 22, 1978.
114. Washington Post, April 25, 1978.
115. Specific details concerning sun's position supplied by Steven Soter, Cornell University Space Science Program; letter to the author, Aug. 2, 1984.
116. Washington Post, April 30, 1978.
117. New York Times, April 21, 1978.
118. Washington Post, April 25, 1978.
119. Ibid.
120. New York Times, April 26, 1978.
121. New York Times, April 24, 1978.
122. New York Times, April 23, 1978.
123. New York Times, April 25, 1978.
124. The Nation, September 24, 1983.
125. Pearson, op. cit.
126. Denver Post, September 13, 1983.
127. Ibid.
128. Washington Post, September 4, 1983.
129. New York Times, September 10, 1983.
130. New York Times, September 14, 1983.
131. New York Times, September 11, 1983.
132. Washington Post, September 4, 1983.
133. New York Times, September 12, 1983.
134. Braunberg, op. cit.
135. Washington Post, September 11, 1983.
136. New York Times, September 2, 1983.
137. New York Times, September 5, 1983.
138. New York Times, September 4, 1983.
139. New York Times, October 7, 1983.
140. New York Times, September 11, 1983.
141. New York Times, September 10, 1983.
142. New York Times, September 2, 1983.
143. New York Times, September 24, 1983.
144. New York Times, August 14, 1981.
145. New York Times, September 10, 1983.

146. Denver Post, September 13, 1983.

147. Manchester Guardian Weekly, February 12, 1984, from the Washington Post.

148. Denver Post, September 13, 1983.

149. Manchester Guardian Weekly, February 12, 1984, from the Washington Post.

150. New York Times Book Review, August 1, 1982.

151. Theodore C. Sorenson. *Kennedy* (New York: Bantam Books edition, 1966), p. 764.

152. Robert F. Kennedy. *Thirteen Days* (New York: New American Library, 1969), p. 68.

153. Henry Fairlie. *The Kennedy Promise* (New York: Doubleday, 1973), p. 311.

154. New York Times, August 19, 1980.

155. As quoted by Tom Wicker, *New York Times*, August 24, 1980.

156. New York Times, November 2, 1982.

157. Colin Gray and Keith Payne, "Victory is Possible," *Foreign Policy*, Summer, 1980.

158. L. FLetcher Prouty. *The Secret Team* (New York: Ballantine Books, 1973), p. 423.

159. Ibid., p. 425.

160. Ibid., p. 429.

161. New York Times, Oct. 7, 1984.

162. New York Times, Oct. 10, 1984.

163. New York Times, Oct. 7, 1984.

164. New York Times, Oct. 10, 1984.

165. New York Times, August 23, 1982.

166. George F. Kennan. *The Nuclear Delusion* (New York: Pantheon Books, 1982), p. 111.

167. Department of State, Justice, and Commerce Appropriations for 1955, Hearings before the House Committee on Appropriations, 83 Cong. 2 sess., p. 125.

168. New York Times, August 2, 1963.

169. Department of State Bulletin, January 6, 1964, Vol. 50, p. 16.

170. New York Times, April 8, 1965.

171. Wall Street Journal, March 5, 1965.

172. New York Times, March 8, 1965.

173. Lin Piao, "Long Live the Victory of the People's War," Peking Review, September 3, 1965.

174. New York Times, February 5, 1983.

175. Ibid.

176. Roger Morris. *Uncertain Greatness* (New York: Harper and Row, 1977), p. 208.

177. Edward Crankshaw. *Moscow v. Pekin* (Middlesex, England: Penguin Books, 1963), p. 84.

178. Ibid., p. 86.

179. Sorenson, op. cit., p. 730.

180. John F. Kennedy, Public Papers, 1963, 459–64.

181. Richard J. Barnet. *The Giants* (New York: Simon and Schuster, 1977), p. 24.

182. Arthur M. Schlesinger, Jr. *A Thousand Days* (Boston: Houghton Mifflin, 1965), p. 904.

183. U.S. Senate Hearings, August 27, 1963, pp. 274–5.

184. Ibid., p. 105.

185. Thomas Powers, "What Is It About?", *Atlantic Monthly*, January 1984.

186. Quoted by Flora Lewis, New York Times, January 6, 1984.

187. Address by George F. Kennan, May 19, 1981.

188. From the film, "War Without Winners."

189. Address by George F. Kennan, May 19, 1981.